The Ultimate Dealer Guide to Facebook Advertising

AMIR RAZAVI

No part of this publication may be reproduced or transmitted in any form or by any means, mechanical or electronic, including photocopying and recording, or by any information storage or retrieval system, without permission in writing from the copyright holder (except by a reviewer, who may quote brief passages and/or show brief video clips in a review)

Disclaimer: The Publisher and the Author make no representations or warranties with respect to the accuracy or completeness of the contents of this work and specifically disclaim all warranties, including without limitation warranties of fitness for a particular purpose. No warranty may be created or extended by sales or promotional materials. The advice and strategies contained herein may not be suitable for every situation. This work is sold with the understanding that the Publisher is not engaged in rendering legal, accounting, or other professional services. If professional assistance is required, the services of a competent professional person, such as the author, should be sought. Neither the publisher nor the Author shall be liable for damages arising herefrom. The fact that an organization or website referred to in this work as a citation and/or a potential source of further information does not mean that the Author or the Publisher endorses the information the organizations or websites may provide or recommendations it may make. Further, readers should be aware that Internet websites listed in this work may have changed or disappeared between the time this work was written and when it is read.

Library of Congress-in-Publication Data

Library of Congress Control Number: 2017904888

Printed in the United States of America

DEDICATION

To my mentors: Tony K. & Alex A. Thank you!

CONTENTS

Acknowledgments   vii

Introduction   9

1 Getting Started with Facebook Ads   13

2 Creating a Buyer Persona   24

3 How to Create Your First Ad   35

4 Facebook Image Guidelines   45

5 Facebook Audience Targeting   50

6 Custom Audiences   61

7 Setting Bids and Budgeting   71

8 CPA and the Different Types of Ad Campaigns   80

9 Facebook Remarketing   90

10 Top Tips for Using Facebook Ads Effectively   99

11 What About Content Marketing?   108

12 Troubleshooting Your Facebook Ads   118

13 Conclusion and Summary   124

ACKNOWLEDGMENTS

Mike S. for introducing me to the industry. Bobby B. and Ehab A. for giving me the opportunity and fine tuning the system. Thank you!

The hundreds of dealers I have worked with over the years, who trusted my knowledge and strategies to help their dealerships grow and succeed. I am always grateful for your continued support. Thank you!

To my team at Get My Auto and RMG, who supported me and continue to support me in our journey of accomplishing our mission of helping dealerships grow and succeed. Thank you!

My various mentors, coaches, peers and friends who have supported me during my journey. We missed out on some fun times while I was focused on building the company, but you still supported me. Thank you!

Introduction

There's an important concept in marketing: Above all else, you have to *be where your customers are*. In today's world, of course, that means being present on the Internet, and on social media sites in particular. This is where buyers do research. It's where they seek information. And it's where they connect—not only with other people, but with businesses and brands. If you want to market effectively, you have to meet your customers where they are, and that means being ready and able to connect with them on social media.

The Influence of Facebook

Critically, not all social media platforms are created equal. Your dealership might or it might not benefit from Twitter, Instagram, Snapchat, or countless other channels. However, the one non-negotiable—the long-tenured king of social media—is Facebook. Facebook is both the largest social media site in the world and the one that offers the most sophisticated suite of marketing tools. For dealerships seeking to sell directly to buyers—establishing a powerful rapport along the way, earning confidence and trust—Facebook is invaluable.

To get a sense of just how influential Facebook is, consider a few quick statistics:

- In the U.S. alone, there are more than 191 million Facebook users.
- The total percentage of the global population using Facebook is more than 22 percent.
- Globally, there are 1.15 billion mobile-only Facebook users each month.
- Annual Facebook advertising revenue exceeds $26.9 billion.

Reaching Buyers on Facebook

Clearly, Facebook is an expansive and important marketing platform for auto dealerships. As you consider how you can use Facebook most effectively, it's important to think in terms of two broad categories—organic reach and paid reach.

- Organic reach refers to the users you connect with simply through providing compelling content on your Facebook account. This will not be the primary focus of this book, but it is important to note that regular content updates are *essential* for a successful Facebook marketing campaign. You use your dealership's Facebook account to share the latest news, products, and promotions, but you can also provide helpful information about the auto buying and auto maintenance processes—a critical way to build authority, to show buyers that they can *trust* you.
- Paid reach, meanwhile, refers to the impressions garnered through Facebook's robust advertising network. This will be the primary focus of this book.

The bottom line for dealerships is that Facebook is a popular destination for people seeking to *connect*—and as such, it provides an invaluable opportunity for your dealership. You can connect with potential customers through both organic and paid means, and in doing so become the dealership *of choice* among your target audience.

Introducing Facebook Ads

The critical point about Facebook, and what dealers need to know, is that it's not just a place to mix and mingle with potential customers; you don't have to simply create a page and hope that customers will come to you. Frankly, this isn't going to work. The good news is that Facebook provides tools for you to reach car buyers *directly*—and not only that, but it allows you to target your advertising efforts so precisely that you're only positing your ads to the people who are actually *likely to buy a car from you.*

Specifically, Facebook provides dealerships with the tools they need to finely segment their audience and reach out to just specific sub-sections of it, ensuring that you're only spending ad dollars to reach the right kind of person—the person looking to buy the specific type of vehicle you're selling. Facebook also provides tools for you to convert those cold leads into warm leads, and from there into customers, keeping each individual highly engaged with your dealership along the way.

The benefits of Facebook Ads go on from there. Not only can you exert tight control over your ad targeting, but you can also exert tight control over your ad budget—allowing you to scale your Facebook Ads campaign as you become more familiar with the platform, and as your dealership itself grows.

What's more, there are innumerable advanced features, including CPA, plus external tools that help you to truly exploit the possibilities of Facebook Ads, and generate incredible returns on your marketing investment.

Crucially, though, Facebook Ads is only as effective as the person using it. The success or failure of your Facebook Ads campaign hinges not on the platform itself, but on the strategy you bring to it. That's what we'll be covering for the remainder of this book—the best ways for you to develop a strategy, to get started on your campaign, and to create a firm foundation for a successful Facebook Ads approach.

What You Will Learn

In this book, you'll learn not just the *what* but the *how* of Facebook Ads—everything the platform will empower you to do, but also how you can obtain the optimal results from it.

As for some of the specific principles and practices we'll cover here, these are just a few of the concepts you will learn:

- How to begin by creating a truly compelling, well-optimized Facebook page for your dealership.
- How to research your audience and to create a "buyer persona," and how that buyer persona can guide your Facebook Ads endeavors.
- How to create your very first ad.
- How to choose between all the different types of ads that Facebook offers.

- How to track your progress, mine your analytics, and ensure that you are on the right track for provable ROI.
- How to use the most advanced and sophisticated Facebook Ads features, including targeting and CPA.
- How to budget properly and prudently.
- And much more!

What we hope is that, once you finish this book, you will feel fully confident in building a new Facebook Ads campaign from scratch, then leveraging it to connect with buyers and start moving inventory— turning your dealership into a powerful, highly-trusted brand, in the process.

Chapter 1
Getting Started with Facebook Ads

Facebook Ads isn't something your dealership can jump into straight away. There are some preliminary pieces of marketing collateral you'll need to develop first, and that includes buyer personas. We'll talk about that in a later chapter.

For now, there is a step even more foundational, and that's actually establishing your dealership's Facebook page. You'll obviously need an account for your dealership in order to take advantage of *any* of Facebook's marketing tools—including content sharing as well as Facebook Ads.

This isn't something to rush, either. Your dealership's Facebook page isn't just an online placeholder. Remember that many buyers will discover your dealership, *through* its Facebook page—meaning the Facebook page establishes first impressions and sets the tone for how people perceive your dealership. In a very real way, your Facebook page is the virtual storefront for your dealership.

In this chapter, we'll provide detailed instructions for creating a Facebook page for your dealership, but also some strategies for *optimizing* that page and ensuring it has appeal for potential customers.

Creating Your Branded Facebook Page

Creating a Facebook page for your dealership requires you to follow a few basic steps; most of these steps can be carried out quite quickly, but you'll want to be sure you're thinking them through and approaching them strategically.

Choose a Classification for Your Dealership

To begin the process of creating a Facebook business page, go to https://www.facebook.com/pages/create.php. Once you're there, you will be greeted with your first choice—a choice between six different classifications for your business. Those classifications include:

1. Local Business or Place
2. Company, Organization, or Institution
3. Brand or Product
4. Artist, Band, or Public Figure
5. Entertainment
6. Cause or Community

Now, when creating a page for your dealership, you'll want to select the first option—Local Business or Place. From there, you'll be given the opportunity to fill in a few additional categories of information. These include:

- About
- Hours
- Contact
- Address
- Price Range
- Parking

Fill out this information as best you can, but don't worry: It's easy enough to make revisions later on, and we'll provide some specific pointers for truly optimizing this basic profile information later in this chapter.

For now, something to concern yourself with is filling in the *next* required field—your business name. You'll want to be careful here, as you are only allowed to change it once, and doing so can be incredibly cumbersome and difficult. Our best advice is to ensure that you state your business name *consistently* across the Internet—meaning that you list it the exact same way on your website, on Facebook, on Twitter, and in any online directories you're listed in. This consistency is necessary for getting maximal SEO value from each listing, and it also avoids any potential confusion from your customers.

For example: If your dealership is called Al's Used Car Company, make sure you spell it out that way *everywhere*; don't take shortcuts by calling it Al's Used Car Co on your website and then Al's Used Cars on Facebook. (It is similarly important to be consistent in how you list your address and other contact information; if you list your dealership location as 123 Main Street on your website, don't list it as 123 Main St. on your Facebook page.)

Finish Your Basic Profile

After you select your business name, Facebook will guide you through some additional profile fields to fill in.

The About Section

First is the About section, specifically a Short Description. This is a brief biography of your company; you might also think of it as an elevator pitch. Essentially, it's the description that people will see on your main page, and it should provide a succinct statement of what makes your dealership special and what value it provides to customers.

We recommend keeping this section to two or three sentences, and also making sure that it includes a link to your dealership's website. We'll have more specifics on this at the end of the chapter.

Note that, as you complete your About section, you'll also have an opportunity to choose your unique Facebook domain—e.g., facebook/com/YourBusinessName. Like your main company name, you'll only have one shot to change this, and doing so isn't easy, so make sure you pick the right domain here! If at all possible, keep it consistent with your business name—so, to return to our earlier example, something like facebook/com/AlsUsedCarCompany might be ideal.

Your Profile Picture

Once you complete these steps, Facebook will prompt you to select a profile picture for your dealership. This will be the primary visual representation of your dealership to Facebook users, though of course, you can change it any time you want. We recommend an image of 180 by 180 pixels, but anything that's a perfect square will probably look just fine. Of course, simply in the interest of appearing professional, your image needs to be suitably clear—nothing blurry or out of focus.

Favorites

The next step is purely a matter of personal convenience. Each individual Facebook user has a vertical bar of "favorite" pages they can easily access, and if you want to add your dealership's page to that menu—allowing yourself to get to it quickly and easily from your Web browser—now is an opportunity to do so. This is strictly up to you, and it doesn't have any real consequence for your dealership marketing.

Your First Ad?

Finally, Facebook will invite you to reach more people by creating your first ad. While using Facebook Ads is our ultimate goal here, we'd recommend skipping this step for now, until you have a better handle on your Facebook marketing plan. But don't worry: We will return to the topic of your first ad later in this book!

Get to Know the Admin Panel

At this point, your dealership's Facebook page is technically live, and in fact you will be given an opportunity to "like" the page from your personal account. Avoid doing so for right now, as liking it may cause it to show up in the newsfeeds of your Facebook friends—and your dealership's Facebook page isn't yet ready for its public debut!

Instead, spend a few moments exploring the options Facebook provides you. At the top navigation bar you should see an option for Settings. Click it, and on the left side of your browser window you should see a vertical navigation bar appear. Here there are several different options that are worth exploring:

- Page Info: Here, you can input some additional information about your dealership, including some options you didn't see in the previous steps.
- Notifications: Here, you'll be able to set the frequency for updates you receive about your page. This is another matter of personal preference; choose whatever option seems most helpful and appealing to you, and don't hesitate to change it any time you like.

- Page Roles: This option will allow you to provide administrative powers to other people within your dealership, people who may need to have their own ability to modify the Facebook page. Be careful not to give these administrative abilities to anyone who you don't absolutely trust with the integrity of your brand, but do give them to any marketing team members or support representatives who you feel need to be involved in your Facebook marketing.

Note that there are a few different Facebook roles you can assign to people, including Analyst, Advertiser, and more. For the purposes of your dealership, Admin is the one role you'll probably want to consider.

Start Sharing Content

Your next step is to actually start using your Facebook page to disseminate some information! You'll definitely want to get some content online before you truly take the page public and encourage other people to like/follow it.

Create Some Posts

Hopefully, you'll make time to add new Facebook posts on a regular basis—ideally every day. For now, though, adding just a couple of posts can be a good start, and an important way to keep your dealership's Facebook page from looking bare and skeletal.

There are six different kinds of Facebook posts to choose from:

1. A text update
2. A photo with caption
3. A link with caption
4. A video with caption
5. An Event page
6. A location check-in

For now, anyway, you'll probably only need to worry about the first four on that list. As for some basics of *what* to post, this could be a book topic in and of itself—but here are some rules of thumb we'd urge you to stick to.

- First, remember to employ a variety of promotional and informational content. You can and should use your Facebook page to let buyers know about any new deals, discounts, sales, or promotions, as well as to provide general news and updates about your dealership. It's important to do more than just *advertise* to people, though, so also try to form relationships and build trust by providing content with informational value—tips on vehicle maintenance, articles on how to get affordable auto insurance, video tutorials about how to clean auto upholstery, etc.
- It is also prudent to include a good mix of media—including some articles, some videos, some photos, some infographics, and some just-text updates.
- Remember that not all of this information needs to be original, branded content for your dealership. If you come across a *New York Times* or *Wall Street Journal* article that speaks to your target audience, or a *Huffington Post* blog that provides information relevant to your niche, by all means share them on Facebook!
- Your guiding principle in sharing information on Facebook should be: Does this provide *value* to my target audience? Is this something that helps them or addresses their needs? If not, then it probably won't help your brand to share it.

Upload a Cover Photo

In addition to a profile picture, you should also upload a cover image— a larger, horizontal image that's displayed at the top of your dealership's Facebook page. The official dimensions for a good, clear cover photo are 851 x 315 pixels. The cover photo should be a branded image, and it can include text on it to invite people to check out your dealership. Of course, this shouldn't be a variation on your cover photo; it's fine to have your dealership logo for the profile picture, for instance, but you don't *also* need to use it for your cover photo.

Invite Likes

Once you have some content on your page, the next step is to get some people to like it. You're now ready to like the page yourself, from your personal Facebook page. In addition, we recommend proactively inviting other people to connect to your dealership's Facebook page:

1. Invite your colleagues and co-workers to like the page; this will provide some good initial activity.
2. Invite friends and acquaintances from your personal network who you think will be supportive of the page. Let them know how grateful you are for any engagement they can provide.
3. Finally, invite customers—but only after you've landed some good, initial activity on the page.

This is also the point at which you can publicize your Facebook page on your company website and anywhere else that permits you to include a Facebook link—in an email signature, for instance, or on your Google My Business page.

Learn How to Measure Your Page Growth

One last task that you might do while you're configuring your dealership's Facebook page is to take a moment to get familiar with Facebook's built-in measurement tools. These might provide you with some useful information as you attempt to grow the page and expand its influence.

To see the different metrics available to you, go to the Insights tab in the top navigation bar. Some of the options you will see include:

- Overview: Clicking this option will show you a seven-day snapshot of all the activity on your page, including likes, overall engagement, etc.
- Likes: Here you will see an overview of how your page's fan base is growing. Note, once you begin to use Facebook Ads, this tab will provide you with a helpful breakdown of your paid vs. organic reach.
- Reach: Here you will see the number of people your page reaches on a given day. If there is one day that shows a big spike in activity, check to see what what was posted that day; it

may provide some useful insight into what you need to be doing to drum up page engagement.

- Visits: This last tab basically shows you where traffic to your Facebook page is *coming* from.

With a brand new page, these fields will all be pretty unhelpful—but keep them in mind, and return to them often to see how your dealership's page is performing.

Optimizing Your Dealership's Facebook Page

By following all of the steps above, you'll end up with a dealership Facebook page that is both functional and professional—ready to go with your Facebook Ads campaign. However, we'd also recommend taking a bit of extra time to go through your profile information and augment it as best you can, truly optimizing how your dealership's Facebook page looks and what sort of information it presents to buyers.

Enhancing Your About Section

In particular, you'll want to go back to that About section and make sure it is rich with useful information for potential buyers. Start with the basics: Ensure that your location and your hours of operation are listed as accurately and completely as possible, and make a note to yourself to revisit these profile fields if the information ever changes. Remember that buyers will use your Facebook page as a resource, a hub of information about your dealership—and you don't want to mislead them!

As for the actual *Short Description* text, you'll want to keep it to under 155 characters in order for it to display properly. We'd advise that you focus this section on the value you offer to buyers. Emphasize *what's in it for them*—affordable prices, no-hassle sales representatives, a wide selection, award-winning customer service, or whatever else lies at the center of your value proposition. Again, this is basically a value proposition.

If possible, use some keywords here. Don't overdo it, and don't shoehorn in keywords just for the sake of having them—but if you can include terms like *used car dealership* or *used cars in Orange County*, to name just two examples, that can certainly help your Facebook profile be found by searchers.

In addition to your Short Description, you'll also have a more thorough Company Overview section. You'll have a higher character count to play with here, though we'd recommend keeping it to a reasonable two paragraphs or so. Here you can go into greater detail about what makes your dealership special; you can include some more keywords; and you can once again include a few links—not just to your company website, but perhaps also to your Twitter page, Google My Business account, or any other online assets you may have.

Remember that you can always go back and revise your About section, so give it some thought and then make any modifications you feel would be beneficial.

Implementing a Call to Action Button

Also worth noting: In late 2014, Facebook rolled out a new call to action feature for business pages. This is essentially a button you can add to the top of your dealership's Facebook profile, making it easier for visitors to your page to interact with your dealership. This is something we recommend you take advantage of.

There are seven basic types of call to action, and several of them will quite obviously be irrelevant to your dealership; for example, Book Now is really just for hotels and restaurants, while Use App and Play Game are more for those in the tech sector.

With that said, there are a few options you might consider for your dealership—among them:

- Sign Up: If you want to use your Facebook page to get people to sign up for your mailing list, this is the button you want to select.

- Shop Now: This one is meant for ecommerce stores, though if you have an online catalog of your vehicles, it can be useful.
- Watch Video: You might consider using this call to action button to take users to an introductory video about your dealership. This is a potentially powerful way to make your dealership a little more human and relatable.
- Contact Us: For most dealerships, this is the best option—a contact form that will allow you to capture leads and stay in touch with some of the people who visit your Facebook page.

Calls to action are incredibly important in online marketing, and you'll be reading more about them once we get into Facebook Ads copywriting, in a later chapter. For now, make sure you put this Facebook profile feature to good use.

Pinning Posts

When someone visits your dealership's Facebook page, he or she will see your posts listed in chronological order, starting with the most recent. The exception is when you use a *pinned* post, which will automatically be displayed at the very top of the page. Pinning posts is not necessary, but it can be a savvy move for ensuring newcomers see especially *important* posts—including a welcome video or a post about a current promotion, contest, or sale.

To pin a post, all you have to do is click the arrow in the upper right-hand corner of the menu. A drop-down menu will appear, and you'll have the option of choosing Pin to Top—as simple as that!

A Work in Progress

Of course, your dealership's Facebook profile is never truly set, and we recommend updating and refreshing it often. Change your profile picture and cover image from time to time. Rewrite your profile biography at least once a year or so. Keep an eye on your pinned posts, changing or unpinning them as needed.

Invest in the ongoing work of maintaining a Facebook profile for your dealership—and your Facebook Ads campaign will be all the more effective because of it.

Chapter 2
Creating a Buyer Persona

There is a good rule of thumb for marketers: You never want to try to sell your products to people in general, but rather, you want to sell them to a specific *group* of people. That is, you want to have a particular audience in mind. When you write marketing copy, you want to address it to a subset of the population that shares some common interests, values, or pain points.

This much is certainly true of your efforts with Facebook Ads. If you try an all-things-to-all-people approach, you're unlikely to get results. To make prudent use of your resources, and to ensure that your ads resonate with the desired audience, you first have to define who that audience is.

There are different tools that can be used to do so, and one of the most essential is the buyer persona. We recommend creating buyer personas before you start creating your first Facebook ad—and in this chapter, we'll show you exactly how that is done.

Why Buyer Personas Matter

As you invest time and money in a Facebook Ads campaign, you want to make sure that you're ultimately showcasing your inventory to the right people—people who you can actually convert into paying customers. This means, most generally, *local* buyers who have the *intention* of purchasing a new vehicle.

Conversely, you don't want to spend your advertising dollars reaching people in China if your dealership is in Nebraska; they're not going to become your paying customers, so it's just a waste of your money. Likewise, those who simply aren't in the market for a new vehicle— perhaps those who have *just* purchased a new vehicle, or those who don't drive at all—should also be excluded from your target audience. Again, spending your ad dollars to reach them is fruitless, as it's never going to yield an actual conversion.

A buyer persona is a tool that is used to profile who your targeted buyers actually are. Using a buyer persona, you can fine-tune your ad campaign to where it is speaking *directly*—and only—to these target buyers.

The buyer persona may contain all kinds of information—sex, age range, geographic locale, likes, dislikes, and beyond—and it can inform everything from your ad *copywriting* to your ad *targeting*. Your buyer persona will show you how to position your dealership, which values to emphasize, and which objections you might need to overcome.

In addition to their usefulness in Facebook advertising, buyer personas can also be handy for your sales representatives to have—so the effort you put into creating them can really yield dividends.

Crafting a buyer persona is an essential step, then—but where do you begin?

The Basic Demographics

The first step is to consider some of the most basic demographics—the simplest and clearest ways in which you can categorize your buyers. For the purpose of Facebook Ads, you might look specifically at age, sex, and geography. In addition to these basics, you'll also want to think critically about psychological and behavioral factors—what the buyer is looking for, how he or she received information, etc.

Before we get into the technical realm, though, step back and think big picture: Who buys the cars that you sell? Primarily old people, or young? Primarily the affluent, or those with smaller incomes?

Your answers to these questions will probably be pretty obvious—for the most part. For example, if your dealership primarily sells high-end sports cars, your target buyers are probably going to be on the wealthier side. Knowing this will really come in handy later, as we get into Facebook Ads' targeting functions, as you'll actually have ways to expressly target the more affluent buyers in your area!

In some cases, though, you may struggle to answer these questions. For example, you may feel like your buyers are pretty evenly split between men and women, or between older and younger drivers. In these more difficult cases, how can you ensure that you're crafting a buyer persona that speaks to the right person?

There are different solutions here, starting with market research. Look at the metrics to see who has bought from you in the past, or survey the visitors who come to your dealership. Who seems to be buying from you? And which units do they prefer?

Another method is to look at website analytics, which can also be quite revealing. If you have Google Analytics installed on your dealership website, you can see which locations people are searching from, which pages of your site are most popular, how long people stay on your website, and more. This can provide some helpful insights into where your buyers come from, and which models seem to interest them the most.

The intention of all these questions and all this research is just to get you thinking about *who* buys from you, and to gather some data to help you understand your audience a little bit better. It is important to point out, though, that none of this actually provides you with a buyer persona; that will require a little bit more work still.

The Persona

That's because a buyer persona is not just a list of demographics. It's actually a full, fictional biography. Your buyer persona may have a fictitious name associated with it, a character you've created to represent one segment of your target audience; to that character you might ascribe hobbies, passions, pet peeves... a full background story! The point in writing this little biography is to get inside the head of your buyers, and to learn more about the people to whom you are marketing.

By getting inside the head of your potential buyer, you can learn *why* he or she might ultimately buy from you—what factors he or she will consider in choosing your dealership over the competition. And when you do that, you get a clear sense of *how* to present your dealership.

How to Create a Buyer Persona

After thinking through some demographic basics, you're now ready to start drafting your buyer persona. In this section, we'll show you how—one step at a time.

Make Sure You've Done your Research

We can't emphasize it enough: Your buyer persona should be rooted in real information and actual trends at your dealership, and to suss all of that out may require you to do a bit of research. In addition to the basic methods we listed above, we'd also recommend these strategies:

- Spend some time looking through your contact database to identify any trends that jump out at you—more buyers than you thought from a certain neighborhood, a noticeable preponderance of women over men, etc.
- Gather information from lead-capturing forms on your website. For example, if someone wants to sign up for your dealership newsletter, provide an option for them to list their gender, their home address, etc.
- Consult with your sales team, and ask for any demographic they can provide you with based on their lead generation efforts.

Do Some Interviews

Another step we highly recommend is interviews—a critical way of learning more about the people who buy from you. There are a couple different ways you can do this.

- Start with your existing customer base. This includes both satisfied customers and also those who you know didn't have the best experience with your company. Reach out to them and ask if you can solicit some feedback; ask them what they liked and didn't like about your dealership, why they ultimately chose your brand, and whether they would recommend it to others.

Reach out to these customers on the phone for the best results; you may be amazed at how many are willing to speak with you, as most customers just really want to be heard.

- You might also glean some information from current prospects; train your sales representatives to ask questions and gain useful information from *lookers* and *shoppers* about why they came to your dealership in the first place and what would motivate them to buy a car from you.

As you attempt to get people to agree to interviews, we recommend a few simple strategies:

- If you find that people generally are not willing to speak with you on the phone, you might consider incentivizing them; something as slight as a $5 Starbucks gift card or entry into a VISA drawing can prove plenty enticing.
- Be up front about the fact that it is not a sales call. State from the outset that you're just looking for honest opinions, and that you will *not* be trying to make a sale.
- As you reach out to potential interviewees, make it convenient for them; allow them to pick the day and time, and send them a calendar request so they'll remember.

To be clear, you don't necessarily need to interview 100 people to craft a good buyer persona, although doing so probably wouldn't hurt. Starting with just four or five can be a good beginning, and provide you with some strong, foundational data.

As for what you should be asking in your interviews, here are just a few recommended questions:

1. What is your job role? Your job title?
2. What are some of your day-to-day responsibilities?
3. What are some of the biggest challenges you encounter?
4. How do you learn new information about products/services? About vehicles in particular?
5. Describe your personal demographics; your educational background; your career path.
6. Describe your family situation.

7. What are the top three considerations you make when choosing a new vehicle? The dealership you buy it from?
8. What kind of online research do you do before buying a new vehicle?
9. What are some of the turn-offs that would discourage you from buying from a particular dealership?
10. Describe your most recent auto purchase; what factors went into your decision?

What you are ultimately aiming for, remember, is to learn *who* your buyers are, and *why* they would or wouldn't buy a vehicle from your dealership. All of this information will be invaluable as you write your buyer persona.

Analyze Your Research

We've talked a lot about gathering research, because it is an essential part of the buyer persona process. Once you gather the research, though, your next step is to analyze it. Read through all the raw information you have gathered and isolate the trends—any recurring themes that stand out to you.

The patterns and commonalities that emerge will provide you with the basic framework for writing your buyer persona.

Fill In Your Basic Demographics

Start by giving your persona a name—something like Driver Dan or Car Buyer Carla. From there, you can write down some demographic notes:

- Include some basic background facts—job, career, and family data. Maybe Driver Dan is a young, single professional; he works in a white collar job and is on a career fast track. Maybe Car Buying Carla is a stay-at-home mom with three kids, ages 10, 7, and 5. She's been married for 13 years.
- Next, fill in sex, age, income level, and location. Driver Dan is a fellow, 28 years old, drawing $49,000 each year and living in the city. Car Buying Carla is a lady, of course, somewhere between

29

35 and 39, with a total household income of $98,000. She and her family live in the suburbs.

- Finally, make note of some identifying character traits. Maybe Driver Dan is a fast-talker, has already done a lot of online research when he comes to the dealership, and prefers that you communicate with him over text. Carla is calm and contemplative, hesitant to make a rash decision that will have such a big impact on her family life; phone calls are easiest for her.

Some of this information you'll need to do some guesswork and speculation for, of course, and for some categories a basic range is fine; it's alright to say that Driver Dan is between 25 and 32, for instance. The goal is to come up with a believable person, based on the information you gathered.

Move on to Motivation

After filling in all the demographic information, your next step is to flesh out your buyer persona with some information about *motivation* and *buying intent*. Again, extrapolate from your data as best you can as you think through these behavioral and psychological points. Here are some categories to consider:

- Start with goals. What is your buyer after? Driver Dan might want something that projects a certain image—one that will help him advance his career. Car Buying Carla might be more concerned with keeping her kids safe, minimizing maintenance needs, or curbing gas costs.
- Next, consider challenges. Dan's might be his limited budget, or his limited time for vehicle upkeep. Carla's might be the simple reality that she has a lot of people to transport, and that she needs a lot of room.
- From there, make notes about *what you can do* to meet the needs of these different people. For Dan, you might advertise some sporty vehicles with reasonable price tags; emphasize that you're quick and easy to do business with. For Carla, you can point to the family-friendliness of your dealership, and

underscore your concern for helping her find *just the right vehicle* for her family's needs.

Add Some Specifics

If at all possible, include some real quotes from your interviews in each buyer persona. For example, maybe you had a conversation with a mom who told you that she was "just looking for someone who could help her find a reliable and roomy family car." That would be a good snippet to include in Carla's persona.

Likewise, make a list of common objections. Maybe you interviewed some people who said they wanted to do business with your dealership but found the pricing to be too steep. You can include those types of issues in your buyer personas.

Craft Messaging

Something that's not strictly mandatory, but may prove helpful, is attaching an image to your buyer persona—a stock photo that will help the *persona* to seem more like a real *person*. This can be especially helpful if you're going to distribute buyer personas to your sales representatives—not really related to your Facebook Ads campaign, but certainly not a bad idea, either.

Finally, place some additional notes about messaging. You might even list an elevator pitch for each persona—a sentence or two that summarizes the way you'd present your dealership to them. This elevator pitch might prove useful as you write your ad copy later on.

Negative Buyer Personas

If you do any additional reading on the topic of buyer personas, you may come across a mention of *negative* personas, or *exclusionary* personas as they are sometimes called. These are, quite simply, representations of the people you *don't* want as a customer.

That sounds a little mean-spirited, but all it means is those customers who may be a little too expensive to acquire, or who may be unlikely to provide you with repeat business or referrals. Negative personas have their place, and there is certainly nothing wrong with constructing one, but they're probably not going to do you much good in your Facebook Ads campaign.

A Buyer Persona Example

To help you think strategically about developing buyer personas for your dealership, here's a sample. You might consider using it as a template for crafting your own buyer persona.

Persona Name: New Dad Nicholas

Background:
- Senior Account Manager for a mid-sized advertising firm
- Has worked at the same company for six years and plans to continue there
- Has been married for six years; has one child, still an infant

Demographics:
- Male
- Age range 28-32
- Dual household income of $83,000
- Lives in the suburbs

Identifiers:
- Quiet and calm
- Does a lot of advance research online
- Would prefer to have emails over phone calls

Goals:
- Wants to provide a good, stable life for his family
- Is looking to find a family vehicle that they can grow into

Challenges:
- Has a limited budget
- Due to college debts, has middling credit and would rather not finance
- Needs something spacious but also fuel efficient

What Can You Do?:
- Advertise special discounts for cash buyers
- Emphasize affordable prices
- Showcase vehicles that seat five or more but also get good gas mileage

Quote:
- "I'm looking for something that will work for a family of three, but that will also still be here when we're a family of four or five."

Objections:
- "I want to pay in cash and these cars aren't affordable."
- "These larger vehicles are all gas guzzlers."

Elevator Pitch:
- Al's Used Car Company makes it easy to find a car you can afford, with special promotions for cash buyers and a range of surprisingly economical family cars.

Putting Your Buyer Persona in Action

Your buyer persona is not just an intellectual exercise. It's an invaluable piece of marketing collateral that can help you hone your Facebook Ads endeavors, ensuring that you're putting those ad dollars toward real connections with actual buyers.

In the coming chapters, we'll keep returning to the buyer persona to help guide the rest of these efforts. You will see in our next chapter how knowing your buyer's background, motivation, and common objections can help you to write truly relevant ad copy.

From there, you'll see how the buyer persona informs your choice of image.

Most significantly of all, you'll see how the buyer persona guides your Facebook Ads targeting efforts. Many of the categories contained in your buyer persona—such as geography and age—will directly correspond to the different categories you can use to filter and target your audience. You can even create custom audiences tailored to fit your buyer persona, ensuring that you always know exactly who you are talking to with each ad.

Chapter 3
How to Create Your First Ad

So far, we've mostly been laying a foundation—getting the right marketing collateral in place before we create our first ad. Now at last, that time has come. Once you have optimized your dealership's Facebook page and created a buyer persona (or, ideally, a set of buyer personas), you're ready to begin the work of creating your very first ad!

Basic Terminology

As you log into Facebook and start using the ad function, you'll find that all of Facebook's paid ad options can be broken down into three elements; knowing this terminology will be important moving forward.

- The **campaign** houses all of your Facebook advertising assets. Think of this as the big picture.
- An **ad set**, meanwhile, will come into play if you are targeting different demographics—e.g., if you're running a different ad for each buyer persona you create. Each ad set will reflect a different audience.
- Finally, the **ads** themselves may vary in terms of their imagery, copy, etc., and they are all housed within those ad sets.

Something else to note is that Facebook offers two basic tools for creating ads—the basic Ads Manager and the Power Manager, sometimes called the Power Editor. The Ads Manager is the best option for most companies, but the Power Manager is a good one for large enterprises looking to exert more control over the ads they run. The bulk of this chapter will focus on the Ads Manager, which is probably the tool you want to start with for your dealership, but we'll circle back around to the Power Manager at the end and explain what makes it unique.

With that terminology explained, you're ready to log into Facebook and get going!

Getting Started

To get started, sign into Facebook using whatever account to which you have assigned an Administrator role. (Simply using the account you used to create the page should work just fine.) On the left side of your browser window you should see a heading marked as Pages, with a few different options beneath it—including Pages Feed, Like Pages, and more. The option you want to click on here is the one that says Create Ad.

If you have multiple Facebook pages, you'll then be asked to select the page for which you'd like to create an ad. Obviously, you want to select your dealership's business page here.

From there, Facebook will ask you an important question: What's your marketing objective? This is a key consideration, and one that makes Facebook's Ads Manager great: You actually get to customize the tool to match your particular marketing goals.

You'll see a large number of potential goals listed, but they'll all be grouped into three basic categories. Those three categories include:

Awareness
- Boost your posts
- Promote your page
- Reach people near your business
- Increase brand awareness

Consideration
- Send people to your website
- Get installs of your app
- Raise attendance at your event
- Get video views
- Collect leads for your business

Conversion
- Increase conversions on a website
- Increase engagement in an app
- Get people to claim your offer

- Promote a product catalogue
- Get people to visit your shops

All three of these options represent truly worthy goals. The first one, awareness, is all about boosting the public visibility of your dealership; this is a great option if your dealership is new or if it struggles to get attention amidst all the other dealerships in your area. Consideration is a good option to choose if you're looking to complete a certain goal that doesn't necessarily involve buying a car, at least not directly— getting more website traffic or promoting an event at your dealership, for example. And conversion is probably the best option if what you're really trying to do is just get people to visit your dealership and purchase an automobile.

Depending on the option you select, Facebook may prompt you for additional information, all of which should be fairly straightforward. For example, if you tell them you want to drive more traffic to your website, you will receive a prompt to input the website URL. For some of these ad options, you may not need to input any additional information.

After you decide on the objective of your ad campaign, you'll be asked to select a name for it; this is purely for your own internal purposes, as the name you pick doesn't really matter, but it can be helpful to include the date on it so that you can compare and contrast with any future ad campaigns you make.

Create Your Audience

Next, you'll want to do is to create your audience. (Once you have actually created your first ad, you will have the option of reusing your previous audience.)

The steps involved here include:

1. Determine whether you want to use a custom audience. Generally speaking, this is a useful step, and one that we recommend. We'll say more about custom audiences in a later chapter.

2. The next step is to choose the locations where you want your ad to be shown. Here it's wise to include the city/cities and suburb(s) from where you get your buyers. You can also input certain areas *not* to include, if you so desire.

3. Choose the age, gender, and language options for your ad. This, of course, is based on the information in your buyer persona.

4. Determine the interests of the people you are targeting. This will be based on information that Facebook has gleaned from user profiles. For example, you can choose to show your ads only to people whose interests include *technology*, or for that matter *automotive*.

5. You'll also see a place where you can target people to include one interest AND another—a great way to narrow your audience even further.

Again, we'll discuss custom audiences and targeting a bit more in a later chapter—but for now, these are the basics.

Building Your Ad Set

The next step is to choose the placement of your ads; you can elect to do this manually or to let Facebook do it for you with its Automatic Placement Feature. Choosing the Automatic option will ensure your ads are shown in the best place without you needing to worry about it. This is what Facebook recommends for most users.

Next, set your budget and schedule. Here you can choose a start date and an end date for your ad, or simply have it run continuously. You can also choose the amount of money you want to spend on your ads *per day*; Facebook will also provide verification of your maximum ad spending per week.

Budgeting is something we'll talk about in greater length later in this book. Our advice for now is that, for your very first ad, picking a smaller budget is usually best; once you get a better sense of what you are doing, and of what works and what doesn't work for your dealership, you can increase your daily ad spend and be a bit more aggressive.

Creating Your Ad

When it comes to actually putting the creative work into your ad, there are a few steps you will be asked to take.

1. The first step is to add your media—that is, to select an image to accompany your ad. We'll provide more tips for this later, but for now suffice to say that you want something inviting, and with a clear call to action. Also make note of Facebook's rule that *less than 20 percent* of your total image space can have text on it. Avoid uploading any image that you know to be too text-heavy!

2. Write a headline and a description. The headline should encourage people to click the post, and the description should provide some additional information about the business or promotion. The most essential ingredient here is a call to action, encouraging your reader to take the next step.

3. Choose your destination—the place viewers will go when they click on your ad. You can set this to your main dealership website, or to a special landing page for the product or event you're promoting. Hopefully, you have Google Analytics set up on your destination page, which will provide you with further information to guide your campaign.

4. Make sure that you have not only created a Pixel, but that you also set it to track and measure traffic from your ad. (We'll go into Pixel in great length later in this book.)

With that, you've officially created your first ad! The next steps, of course, are to monitor your results and start thinking about the *next* ad you'll create.

Facebook Power Manager

Before we come to those topics, though, let's revisit the Facebook Power Manager. You'll remember that, thus far, we've been writing about the more basic Facebook Ads Manager, and that this is probably the best option for those who are new to Facebook Ads. If you're more experienced or are looking for something a little more robust, though, you may want to consider Facebook Power Manager.

What is Power Manager?

Basically, Power Manager is a version of Ads Manager that focuses more on bulk actions. It's geared toward people who are running multiple campaigns, multiple ad sets, many different ads. The whole point of it is for advertisers to have an easier time taking multiple actions at once.

Because the people who use Power Manager are, well, "power users," Facebook will usually use this platform to debut new features before they come to the basic Ads Manager.

That's a big upside, but the downside is that it's simply a lot more complicated, especially for novices and for more small-scale advertisers who are generally just focused on one more limited campaign.

The Pros and Cons of Power Manager

There are a few real benefits that Power Manager offers, and it's worth making note of them here: Power Manager makes it easy to make changes to multiple ad campaigns at the same time, or to copy one campaign and use it as the basis for a new one.

With that said, Power Manager can also needlessly complicate the situation, especially tracking the metrics of your campaign. Believe it or not, Power Manager actually makes it more difficult to glean information about your campaign, which means that those who really want to dig into their data are really better off with the basic Ads Manager.

The bottom line is that Power Manager is a tool made primarily for *marketers*—not for those who are simply trying to run some effective ads for their auto dealership. Unless you reach the point where you are a seasoned pro and want to explore all the available options, we recommend just sticking with the basic Ads Manager.

How to Write Amazing Copy for Your Ad

Crafting an effective Facebook ad is part art and part science. We've covered some of the more technical elements of it already—but there is also a need for some real creativity. You've got to write sales copy to accompany your ad, and in many ways that's the most important part of the entire process. The strength of the sales copy you write is what will ultimately make or break your Facebook ad campaign. This encompasses both the copy you write for your headline as well as the body text of your ad.

Writing a Strong Headline

As with all digital marketing copy, the headline is critical; it's what sets first impressions and ultimately determines whether your reader clicks on the link or just keeps scrolling through Facebook. Remember that your ultimate goal in writing a headline is to generate engagement, but *not* to get *everyone* to click your ad; just to get *the right people*—the people for whom your ad is designed—to click it!

As you work on your headline, here are some considerations to make:

- First, go back to your buyer persona. Refresh yourself of the values and pain points you're trying to speak to, and also review the elevator pitch and any other marketing notes you put together. All of this can be invaluable in reminding you of *who you're talking to*, and also of *how to get their attention*. Basically, your buyer persona can help you ensure that you are speaking the same language as your potential buyer.
- Be mindful of the character limit—which for a Facebook ad is just 25 characters! Brevity is obviously going to be key, and you're going to need to do a lot with a little.
- Your headline should ultimately convey value. As you write, put yourself in the shoes of your buyers. Ask yourself *what's in it for them*. How will their life be better off for having clicked your Facebook ad? That's ultimately what your headline should convey.
- It is also important that your headline offer truth in advertising. Don't promise anything you can't deliver, and don't try to do a bait and switch. If your headline claims to be about financing deals, the ad itself should take your reader to a page with

41

clearly-displayed, easy-to-find financing deals. In other words, the phrasing of your headline should be relevant to its actual contents.

- While there is not necessarily a magic formula for great headlines, there are some common practices that are worth trying. One is to make sure your headline leads with a strong action word—*Discover* new cars. *Experience* great deals. These words promote *action* on the part of the reader. A riskier but sometimes valuable alternative is to ask a question in your headline—assuming it's one you believe will be provocative. *Looking for affordable cars? Ready to fall in love with an SUV?*

Writing the Body Text for Your Facebook Ad

When it comes to the body text of your Facebook ad, many of the same rules apply. You still want to speak to pain points. You still want to overcome objections. You still want to convey value. You still want to offer truth in advertising.

You still have a character limit to deal with, too—90 characters in total. That gives you a little bit more wiggle room, but not a lot. You still need to come up with compact messaging.

As for specific tips for your ad copy, here are some recommendations:

- Remember your audience! Not only do you have your buyer persona to consult, but by this point you've already set your Facebook audience—so you know who you're addressing with this copy. Good Facebook ads don't come in one-size-fits-all iterations; you've got to write differently for different people.
- Also remember your visual. The image and the written copy should go together, not create a jarring experience for the reader!
- The best Facebook ads have one clear goal, and copy that reflects that—culminating in a strong call to action. Stay focused, and remember to use those strong action words to promote your reader to do something.
- While 90 characters isn't a lot, you still want to lead with value, coming as quickly as you can to the what's-in-it-for-me part of

your ad. Don't give readers an excuse to stop reading mid-sentence.

- Avoid jargon or overly technical language. You're selling cars, but that doesn't mean your ad copy should talk about catalytic converters or anything that the lay person wouldn't immediately grasp. Focus on benefits; focus on what you're offering, and what the reader should do next.

- Get to the numbers! If you're advertising a specific car, list the price. If you're promoting a big sale, specify the savings that people can get. Numbers are appealing. They grab attention. And being up front about them can help buyers feel more confident clicking your ad.

- If you feel stuck, we recommend taking just a few minutes to scroll through your Facebook newsfeed. Check out the ad copy that other companies are writing. Get a feel for the stylistic choices they make. You might find real inspiration for your own ad!

- Finally, remember that you can and should test ads. Let's say you have new ad copy that you think is really strong. That doesn't mean you should immediately spend $1,000 on it. Start smaller, safer. Facebook Ads will let you budget as much as a single dollar, and while that may be a little *too* low, it's nice to know that Facebook makes it easy for you to test ads on low budgets, seeing what works and what doesn't. If you spend $20 on your new ad and it gets a lot of engagement, that's when you may want to up the ante a bit!

To summarize, the rules of thumb with all your Facebook ad writing copy are to focus on the buyer, and keep everything short, simple, and centered on value.

An Ongoing Process

It's crucial to note that you're never going to arrive at the one perfect piece of Facebook Ads copy that you can simply keep using forever. Eventually, any ad is going to see diminishing returns. There is a constant need to review your ad metrics and to refine the copy as needed. To do this, you will need to not only consult with your Facebook Ads data, but also keep your buyer personas up to date. And as you do make changes to your ad copy, don't forget the value in ongoing testing! Always be on the lookout for an even better, more effective way to fulfill your Facebook Ads goals.

The Next Step in Your Facebook Ads Campaign

This chapter has provided an overview of some of the nuts-and-bolts elements of Facebook Ad creation—but now it's time to dive deeper into a few of the specific skillsets you'll need to make your Facebook Ads campaign a success. This includes image selection, custom audience targeting, budgeting, and beyond.

Chapter 4
Facebook Image Guidelines

We all know the old saying about the worth of pictures, and they are indeed invaluable in communicating your marketing message—especially when you only get 90 characters of text to accompany them. What this means is that, when creating your Facebook ad, it's imperative that you be judicious in your image selection—picking something that looks professional and speaks to high standards of quality, but also something that grabs attention and ultimately entices buyers to stop and see what your ad is all about.

Getting the Right Dimensions

When creating your Facebook ads, you'll have the option to choose the images you wish to accompany them. Depending on the type of ad you've chosen, you'll need to choose images with different dimensions. This section will act as a quick resource to help you find that information.

To begin with, a quick refresher about those images you use on your dealership's Facebook business page—your profile picture and your cover image. For these, the recommended dimensions are 180 x 180 pixels and 828 x 315 pixels, respectively. For the profile picture, note that most any perfectly square image will probably work alright.

As for the images you choose to go with your ads, it all comes down to the type of ad you select. For App Installs/Engagement ads, your image should be 1,200 x 628. For photo ads, the images will need to be 1,200 x 900 and for videos, you'll have to choose a thumbnail image that's 1,200 x 675. Carousel images should be 600 x 600, and website links 1,200 x 628.

Events images should optimally be 1,200 x 444, and lead generation ads 1,200 x 628. Offer claims should likewise be 1,200 x 628, while page likes are 1,200 x 444 again.

Quick Notes About Facebook Image Dimensions

An important note: The display dimensions aren't going to be the same as the actual dimensions – and this will vary from device to device. In other words, an image may appear bigger on a mobile device than it does on a desktop computer. It's worthwhile to view your image on multiple devices before you commit to it, or at least before you put a lot of money behind the ad, so that you can be sure of what it really looks like to buyers.

Note also that Facebook is lenient and you don't need your images to be the *exact* same dimensions as those specified here. That said though, if you want to minimize any warping or stretching, then it is a good idea to aim for images that are as close as possible. At the very least, try to get the aspect ratio right.

High definition images that look crisp are always going to attract more views and clicks than those that look grainy and blurry. Grainy images make your dealership look dated, which in turn makes you look less trustworthy and reduces the likelihood people will want to buy from you.

Choosing the Right Format for Your Facebook Ad

It's also important to briefly comment on the file formats that are acceptable for Facebook ads. Currently, there are three supported file extensions you can use-- .jpg, .png, and .gif images. Chances are, any photos or images your dealership uses for marketing collateral will be in one of these three formats, but it's something you'll want to check and verify before moving ahead.

What's Not Allowed in Facebook Images?

Advertisers should also make note of Facebook's community standards and practices, which govern what is and isn't allowed in ad images.

Chances are, any advertising you try to do for your dealership will conform to these guidelines without any problem—but still, it's important to just be aware of the rules.

A few items that are *not* allowed in your Facebook ads include:

- Anything that advertises or promotes illegal products or services.
- Anything that actively promotes discrimination on the basis of race, ethnicity, color, gender identity, family status, disability, etc.
- Anything that promotes tobacco products or related paraphernalia.
- Anything that promotes the sale or use of drugs or drug-related products.
- Anything that promotes unsafe supplements.
- Anything that promotes weapons, ammunition, or explosives.
- Anything that promotes the sale or use of adult products or services—e.g., products or services for sexual pleasure.
- Adult content of any kind—suggestive sexual content, etc.
- Any ad content that is misleading or false. (This returns to our previous advice about offering truth in advertising.)
- Anything including profanity.

This is a good place to note that whatever ads you submit will be reviewed by Facebook, and they won't run without Facebook's approval—so compliance with these guidelines is critical. Also note that the Facebook Ads team will most likely turn down any ad submissions that link to non-functional landing pages or that include bad grammar/poor spelling.

Tips for Choosing Your Facebook Ad Images

There is, of course, a world of difference between picking an *acceptable* image for your Facebook ad and picking an *optimal* one. Just as your headline is essential for setting a strong first impression and encouraging buyers to take note, your image can command attention and draw more eyeballs to the offer you're making.

So how do you ensure that your Facebook ad image is truly a good and effective one? First, we should emphasize once again the importance of testing. The only way to know for sure that an ad image is compelling is to try it out, starting with a more limited budget and then ultimately with a few more ad dollars behind it. A/B testing can be useful here; use the same ad copy but two different images, run both ads at the same time, and see if one engenders significantly more engagement than the other. Also, keep track of the images that work best for you, and look to identify trends; if all your more successful ads include pictures of sports cars, that tells you something about what your audience likes.

Here are a few additional strategies that we'd recommend for choosing the right Facebook ad image.

- Remember that a lot of people will view your ad while scrolling through their Facebook feed, sometimes on their smart phone or their mobile device. What this means is that you shouldn't opt for anything too intricate, or anything with a lot of small details. Instead pick something that is bright and eye-catching—something that will be immediately identifiable to anyone who is simply scrolling along.
- The image should also be somehow related to your dealership—to the products and services you offer. Remember what we have already said about the importance of truth in advertising, and the dangers in "bait and switch" tactics. Using an image of the latest video game system, or of a controversial celebrity, just to get eyeballs on your ad, probably won't build much trust or generate many sales.
- With that said, there are some creative directions you can go in. Pictures of people's faces tend to get attention, and *happy* faces are especially useful—e.g., the happy faces of satisfied buyers as they get the keys to their new vehicle!
- We also recommend choosing colors that stand out. This does not mean opting for something neon or garish. What it means is recognizing that Facebook's own color scheme is blue and white—and if you want your ad to stand out rather than fade into the background, we'd recommend picking a different set of colors than that.
- Including your logo somewhere in the image can also be smart; it may not lead to a lot of conversions right away, as it's not as eye-catching as the picture of a happy customer or a beautiful car, but it *will* improve brand visibility, and over time it can help create familiarity and trust.

- Your image can also include a value proposition. Are you offering a free extended warranty, or some other such add-on? Including a word like "free" in your ad—assuming you don't make it too large—can really grab attention!
- Humor tends to work well in Facebook ads, too—so if there is a way for you to develop a funny image that still reflects your dealership's actual product and service offerings, that's certainly worth trying.

Final Thoughts on Facebook Images

The image you choose for your Facebook ad is critically important—and there are a number of considerations you have to keep in mind. Your image needs to have the right dimensions, lest it look unclear or distorted. It needs to comply with Facebook's code of conduct. And it needs to be something that draws attention to itself while still truthfully representing your dealership's value proposition.

This is a lot to think about, so take some time in strategizing about the right imagery—and don't forget to do some testing! Discovering the best kind of image for your dealership will make your Facebook ads infinitely more effective.

Chapter 5
Facebook Audience Targeting

We've circled around the concept of audience targeting, and now at last it's time to discuss it in earnest. The ability to precisely target *who* you are running ads for is one of the very best reasons to use Facebook Ads—one of the distinctions that makes it a top-tier marketing tool, and a must for your dealership.

To put it a little differently, if you use Facebook Ads but don't take advantage of the Audience Targeting functionality, you're not getting the maximum bang for buck; you're not using this platform for all it can do. Audience Targeting allows you to speak directly to *local buyers* who have shown *an intention to purchase a new vehicle*—in other words, just the sort of people who are most likely to read and respond favorably to your ad. By targeting with precision, you can boost the efficacy of your ad copy by marrying it to the proper reader, and you can also get more value from your advertising dollars; instead of spending money advertising to the general public, you can spend money advertising to the people who might actually become paying customers. Targeting is the best method of creating efficiency in your advertising budget.

So how do you get started? When creating your ad in the Facebook Ad Manager, there is a section called *detailed targeting*. This is where you get to choose *exactly* who you want to share your ads with and this will allow you to choose from a rather massive list of factors. These include:

Demographics
- Education
- Ethnic affinity
- Financial
- Generation
- Home
- Life Events
- Parents
- Politics
- Relationships

- Work

Interests
- The list here is simply sprawling, even too much to be summarized, and for the most part dealerships will want to stick with the Behaviors classification anyway.

Behaviors
- Automotive
- Behaviors
- Behaviors targeting
- Charitable donations
- Buyer classification
- Digital activities
- Expats
- Financial
- Mobile device user
- Network connection
- Purchase behavior
- Residential profiles
- Seasonal and events
- Travel

There are more besides—but you get the idea. Of course, some of these targeting categories are fairly self-explanatory; you might see immediately how they could relate to your dealership's advertising endeavors. Others may be a little more opaque to you. Of course, not all of these categories are going to be relevant to your dealership, so if there is one that you don't think fits or doesn't make much sense, well, you're probably right. There is certainly no need to grapple with each and every one of these categories in your dealership's Facebook advertising.

The key is to be strategic and to think about who is *really* likely to want your product – and sometimes, this might mean taking into consideration some surprising factors.

Here is just one example. Say you were selling a weights bench. In this case, you might choose to show it to bodybuilders who also happen to be homeowners. This would take you down this trail: Behaviors > Residential profiles. Why? Because they're much more likely to have the space to keep something so big, versus someone who is renting a small apartment.

Using the Facebook Audience Targeting Tool

Note that there are a couple of subtleties to be aware of when using this section. When you list the qualities you are looking for in your users, note that these are not necessary requirements. If you put everything into the top box, then your ads will show to people who tick any of those boxes.

But if you click *Filter* and *Narrow* just below, then you get two more boxes. One says 'and MUST ALSO match at least ONE of the following.' This allows you to string together different targeting criteria, to hone your search to people who fall into various overlapping categories. This is how you would make sure that your audience includes people who are both bodybuilders *and* homeowners, as opposed to showing your ads to *bodybuilders* as well as to *homeowners*. This is a subtle distinction, but a critical one, showing your weight bench ad to homeowners who are not also bodybuilders would obviously be limited in its helpfulness.

Likewise, you can use the filter section to exclude people from your ads. This is the section that says 'EXCLUDE people who match at least ONE of the following.'

So this way, you could exclude women for instance, in order to target your product *only* at men. If you have product that is designed for people on a more frugal or restrictive budget, then you could look at Behaviors > Buyer profiles > High spenders and use this to exclude people who prefer high-end, premium products.

Using all these tricks, you can get inside the head of your buyer and then make sure that they *specifically* see your ad. Of course, this requires some familiarity with all of the different filters and categories that Facebook provides; the best way to gain that familiarity is, frankly, by just spending some time exploring. It doesn't cost you anything to just click around through the different lists to see all of the available options, and to think through how each option might be relevant to your dealership.

Facebook Local Awareness

In a moment, we will offer some specific tips for using these audience targeting functions to segment your audience—but first, it's important to discuss a separate but related feature, Local Awareness.

Your dealership is a local entity, and it doesn't do you much good to display ads for buyers in *Indonesia* when your inventory is all in *Indiana*—and that's true no matter how precisely you use the Audience Targeting functions. It is imperative to wed your behavioral/demographic targeting with geographic targeting—and frustratingly, this requires you to head to another section of Ad Manager, called Local Awareness.

To do this, simply create an ad campaign as you normally would, using the tips we've covered in previous chapters, but then look for the option in the left hand menu that is called *Local Awareness*. Click this and you'll be shown a map and a search bar. You can now search for your local area using the town, city, state, or ZIP code. You'll then be given the option to choose a radius—so, for example, you can pinpoint your dealership's location and choose only to advertise to buyers who are within five miles, 25 miles, 50 miles, etc.

Choosing the radius you want really boils down to the kind of competition you have; if you're one of the only dealerships in the area, and there are many surrounding suburbs where buyers would likely drive several miles to come to you, then a larger radius might make sense. In a more competitive market, it might make more sense to focus on your more immediate neighborhood. Remember that the more precise you can be here, the fewer wasted ad clicks you will get. Also note that Facebook makes it possible for you to target your ads *very* narrowly; in fact, you can choose to show your ads only to those who are within a single mile of your dealership! (50 miles, meanwhile, is the maximum.)

Additional Features within Facebook Local Awareness

In addition to selecting a location, Facebook Local Awareness also gives you the ability to choose whether or not you reach *everyone* in that location, or just a subset; the available subsets include:

- People who live in the location
- People who have recently been in the location
- People who are traveling through the location

Another important feature that Local Awareness ads offer: the ability to add some unique calls-to-action that are *only* available for these locally-focused ads. Some of these options include Get Directions, Call Now, and Message, all three of which can be invaluable ways to connect with nearby buyers who happen upon one of your dealership's ads. Using these calls to action can be an optimal way to boost ad engagement.

One more note about Local Awareness: It will automatically optimize your ads for Daily Unique Reach. What this means is that it will show your ad to any given Facebook user only once daily, rather than inundating a single user with the same ad over and over again.

Tips for Targeting Your Facebook Ads

We noted above that there are many different options available for targeting your Facebook ads—some of which may be highly relevant to your dealership, some of which may not be relevant at all. Frankly, this can all be daunting, especially to those who are new to Facebook Ads.

The good news is, you don't have to overthink your options,and sometimes the simplest solution really is the best. What we recommend is targeting this way: Behaviors > Automotive. This will show your ads to those who have displayed an intention to purchase a new vehicle— and that, of course, is who you want to reach. There are other ways you could target your ads, but this is the simplest way, and a highly effective one.

You might be wondering: How does Facebook know whether a person is looking to buy a new car or not? This is where we get into some of the truly brilliant, data-driven services that Facebook offers. Specifically, Facebook has access to data gathered by the marketing and analytics group Polk, which sources US consumer household information from DMVs, vehicle registration data, etc. This information is incredibly accurate, because, again, it's based on actual vehicle registration numbers in *your* specified location.

New vs. Used Cars

Within the Automotive Behavior section, your dealership can select different sub-behaviors that correspond with the vehicles you're selling. For example, you may target your ads to different buyers depending on whether you are selling new or used vehicles.

Let's assume you are selling new cars. If that's the case, you can select either *New Vehicle Shoppers (in market)* or *New Vehicle Shoppers (Max in market)*. That one word actually makes quite a bit of difference: *Max in market* buyers are looking to procure their new vehicle within 90 days, while those who are simply *in market* have a timespan of twice that long, 180 days. In other words, going max in market gets you hotter leads.

That's not to say that it is always the better option, however. There are tradeoffs to consider. Selecting *Max in market* will allow you to specify the type of vehicle the buyer is looking for—an SUV, for example, or a sedan. If you just choose *in market*, meanwhile, Facebook will actually allow you to specify a particular brand.

So which of these options is better for your dealership? Well, this is where testing can be essential. This is the only way to really know for sure what kind of targeting generates the best results for your dealership.

Other Targeting Options

Beyond the used car and new car distinction, there are some other ways in which Facebook Ads allows you to sub-target your efforts. There are three in particular that are worth noting, all of them available under the Automotive Behavior category.

1. **Owner.** This option allows you to find someone who purchased a car several years ago and may be looking for an upgrade, just as an example.
2. **Income.** If you are selling luxury vehicles or sports cars, you may wish to target your ads to people with high income levels-- $100,000 or above. If your ads emphasize the affordability of your automobiles, meanwhile, denoting a lower income level might make more sense. Again, this just varies according to the particulars of your dealership.
3. **Make:** If your dealership sells just one make of automobile, or if you're looking to move a particular kind of inventory, this can certainly be a helpful option. A new Toyota dealership, for instance, might target those who are specifically looking for a Toyota.

These options represent a *beginning*—and once again, we can't emphasize enough the importance of thorough testing. Put a few advertising dollars behind some different options, track your results, see what works and what doesn't. That's the best way to get a feel for the kind of targeting you need to be doing for your car dealership.

Motorcycles

If your dealership happens to sell motorcycles, you might be encouraged to know that Facebook has some targeting options just for you. To access them, go back to the beginning of our targeting discussion, where we selected Behaviors > Automotive. There, in addition to the *New vehicle buyers (in market)* and *New vehicle buyers (Max in market)* options, you'll also see a choice for *Motorcycles*.

Once you are there within the Motorcycle sub-category, you'll have another couple of options to pick from—*Purchased* and *Owners*.

Choosing the *Owners* sub-category will allow you to target people according to the type of motorcycle they own; you'll have some options for specific brands, like Harley and Kawasaki, but also choices such as *Domestic* brands, *All-Terrain Vehicles*, motorcycles with *Less than*

600cc Engine, Minibike/Moped/Scooter, Off-Road/Trail/Dirt Bike, and more.

Meanwhile, if you choose the *Purchased* category, you'll get to choose buyers according to how recently they bought their motorcycle (0-6 months ago, 7-12 months ago, over 48 months ago, etc.) and also whether they purchased it new or used.

Using these different options and features, you can reach out to motorcycle lovers who may be in the mood to upgrade their existing bike; again, a little testing can help you figure out which options make the most sense.

Aftermarket

The Automotive Behaviors section will also allow you to choose the *Owners* subcategory, and there you'll have a number of options about *where/how* the individual purchased his or her vehicle. These options include:

- Aftermarket
- Make
- Purchased
- Style
- Vehicle Age
- Vehicle Price

The aftermarket option is a good one to note here, because it's a valuable way to target vehicle owners who are likely to buy additional parts, services, or accessories for their vehicle. If your dealership offers these, this can be a fruitful avenue of targeted advertising. In fact, there are three basic subsections you can choose here:

- Auto Parts
- Auto Parts and Accessories
- Auto Service Buyer

Pick the option that best fits what your dealership's parts and service center offers.

Purchased

The *Purchased* targeting option, meanwhile, allows you to specify how recently your targeted buyers obtained their current vehicles. The options include:

- 0-6 months ago
- 7-12 months ago
- 13-24 months ago
- 25-36 months ago
- 37-48 months ago
- Over 48 months ago

There are different ways you can put these filters to use—for instance, singling out buyers who have owned their cars for a longer span of time and might therefore be ready for an upgrade or a change.

Style

Simply put, this targeting category allows you to target potential buyers based on the style of vehicle they currently own—including such options as Commercial Truck, Crossover, Economy/Compact, Full-Size SUV, and Full-Size Sedan.

Often, vehicle owners will be fairly committed to a particular style, so you may find value in targeting those who already own a vehicle in the same style as the ones you are promoting.

Vehicle Age

This is an option fairly similar to the *Purchased* option, only here you'll be targeting according to the actual age of the vehicle, not necessarily how recently it was purchased. The utility of this feature is much the same, however—selecting buyers whose vehicle is in the 11-15 year or 16-20-year range can help you to speak directly to those who probably *need* an affordable new car very badly.

Vehicle Price

You will also see that Facebook allows you to target buyers based on the vehicle price range they're looking for, a good way of matching your marketing with the budget of your buyers. The options available here include:

- Less than $20,000 (a particularly good option for used car dealerships)
- $20,000-$30,000
- $30,000-$40,000
- $40,000-$50,000
- $50,000-$75,000
- Over $75,000

If Your Targeting Goes Wrong...

We have repeatedly emphasized the role of testing in a Facebook Ads campaign, which in turn underscores an important truth about Facebook advertising—that is, that you won't necessarily nail it on the very first attempt, and that there is always some trial and error involved.

What does it mean, though, if your ads simply aren't getting results, no matter how hard you try? It could very well be the case that you're making some fundamental errors in your targeting.

The most common such error is not targeting *enough*. Remember that the narrower you target, the fewer wasted clicks you will have. Leaving your ads too general, your audience too undefined, will result in ads that just don't land with the right people, and that means wasted money in your marketing budget.

If this is the boat you are in, go back through some of the different criteria we noted above and add some filters to your targeting choices. Really hone in on a specific subset of people, using all of the options and tools that Facebook makes available to you.

Keep at it. Keep targeting. Keep testing. That's how you ensure that your Facebook Ads campaign is truly great.

Facebook Audience Targeting Recapped

The big-picture takeaway for auto dealers is that one of the most important parts of your automotive advertising campaign is *targeting*. It's worth your time to be strategic not just about the contents of your ads, but also the audience for those ads. One of the best routes for doing this is to select Behaviors as your first targeting criteria, then choosing Automotive and narrowing it down from there. Make sure to also specify your location, using Facebook Local Awareness.

Through the right targeting, you can minimize the risk of your ads falling on deaf ears—and ultimately get much more bang for your marketing buck.

Chapter 6
Custom Audiences

We have said repeatedly that Facebook Ads is an incredible platform, packed with a lot of smart and useful tools—tools that most advertisers aren't even aware of, especially newcomers and amateurs. Familiarizing yourself with these tools is a powerful way to establish an edge over your competition—and there are few tools more helpful or more misunderstood than Custom Audiences.

You may remember that we referenced this feature in our chapter about how to build your first ad—but what *is* Facebook's Custom Audiences feature, exactly? Essentially, custom audiences allow you to choose even more precisely who you want to target. Now, after the last chapter, you may be asking: How can you target someone more precisely than choosing their age, location, job, and hobbies?

Would you believe that Facebook allows you to create an actual list of the *specific* individuals to whom you wish to advertise? That's basically what Custom Audiences is.

In this chapter, we'll discuss this feature at length—what it is, why it's important, and how you can use it to make your ad campaign even more finely-honed and effective.

How to Create a Custom Audience

Let's get started by rolling up our sleeves and actually creating a custom audience together. To do this, what you'll need to do is go to Ads Manager (or the Power Manager, if that's the route you've chosen). From there, click on Audiences. You'll find this under the Tools section.

Assuming this is the first Custom Audience you've created, you'll need to select the button that says Create Audience. From there, you'll get a popup window that basically asks you what type of audience you'd like to create.

Types of Custom Audience

There are several different types of Custom Audience you can create, and in fact Facebook is adding to the list all the time. Here are just a few of the options you'll want to know about.

- **Customer List.** This is sometimes just called the *Standard Custom Audience* function. It reflects a list of email addresses, phone numbers, or Facebook user IDs. You can upload your list directly to Facebook and it will match it with existing Facebook users, at least as best as it can; usually, you'll get between 60 and 80 percent matches. (Some of the people on your list may not have Facebook, or they may not have their account synced with the contact information you have on file.)
- **Website Custom Audiences.** Using a Facebook Pixel tracking code (something we'll discuss more in a later chapter), you can target your Facebook Ads to those who have visited your dealership's website within a set period of time—for instance, in the last week, the last month, etc. You can actually go up to 180 days!
- **App Activity Custom Audiences.** If you have an app for your dealership, you can create a Custom Audience based on that activity. We won't say a great deal about this, as most dealerships don't do too much with custom apps.
- **Engagement Custom Audiences.** These are actually based on people who have engaged with your ads in the past. Technically, you can create an audience based on those who have engaged with your ad at any point in the past 365 days. We would generally recommend a more recent time frame, though; the person who hasn't clicked on an ad in 365 days can't really be said to be *engaged* in any meaningful way.

Lookalike Audiences

Another option that's good to know about is the Lookalike Audience. This is an option you will only have available to you once you've created your first Custom Audience. Basically, it involves Facebook looking at your current ad users and buyers to see if any trends or patterns emerge—anything your user base seems to have in common.

This might include age, gender, interests—points you might have overlooked. Using this information, Facebook will create a larger and broader list of users who may have never interacted with your brand before, but who fit the trends of your existing buyers. This can be a useful way to detect buyer patterns you might otherwise have missed, and to create a broader audience for your ads.

How to Create Customer List Custom Audiences

Now, let's take a look at a few of these Custom Audience types in greater detail, and show some of the ways in which you can use them in your dealership's Facebook Ads campaign.

Remember that this is the option allowing you to upload a list of your existing buyers—either by email, phone number, or Facebook user ID. There are two basic ways in which you can do this:

1. Manually upload your list in either a .txt or a .csv format.
2. Sync up with your email CRM, connecting it to your Facebook Ads account.

Manually Uploading Your List

Currently, Facebook *only* offers integration with the MailChimp CRM—which means that there is a decent chance you'll need to manually upload a text file. To make this happen, you'll need to open either Excel or a basic text editing program and create your list one line at a time. Your list should follow this basic pattern:

EmailA@hotmail.com
EmailB@gmail.com
EmailC@aol.com
EmailD@gmail.com
Email@utk.edu

… and so on. Note that you can opt for phone numbers (with area codes) instead of email addresses, and that's totally fine. The one item you can't do is mix data types. Your list must be either all email addresses *or* all phone numbers—not a mixture of the two.

You will also want to provide your Custom Audience with a name; this is strictly for your own internal purposes, so our recommendation is to pick something that's just short and easy to remember. "Former customers" or "auto fair signups" are good examples.

Syncing Your List Automatically

If you do have MailChimp, feel free to select the Custom Audience Sync tool, which will save you time. Facebook will guide you and prompt you through this process one step at a time, so we won't get into it here.

How to Create a Website Custom Audience

The next type of Custom Audience to address is the Website Custom Audience. You will remember that this one involves those buyers who have been to your dealership website lately. This can be a good option for those dealers who just don't have large databases of existing buyers or leads. Indeed, one of the nice features about Website Custom Audiences is that they don't require you to have any information at all.

Install Facebook Pixel

What you do need to do is install Facebook Pixel, which will provide you with a special tracking code. This, in turn, lets Facebook recognize website visitors and automatically add them to an Audience.

We have already mentioned Pixel a couple of times in this book, and we'll devote a later chapter to some more advanced uses for Pixel. For now, let's just go over the quick steps to install and verify it so that you can use it for your Website Custom Audience.

Go to the Pixel tab in Ads Manager—and from there:

1. Click *Create a Pixel.* (Be aware that you can only do one Pixel per account.)
2. Enter a name for it—something that represents your dealership.
3. Check the box to signify that you accept the terms and conditions.

4. Use the Pixel code on all the pages you wish to track. To do this, you may need to talk with your website developer; or, if you use Wordpress for your dealership website, simply download the free plugin Pixel Caffeine, which will handle everything for you.

Note that Pixel doesn't just track visitors to your website; it can also track a number of other "events." We won't get into all of that here.

How to Create an *Advanced* Website Custom Audience

For those who have created some Custom Audiences before and want to fine-tune their targeting a bit, Facebook has started offering an advanced mode; if you're still new to Custom Audiences, we'd recommend just skipping this section for now.

Basically, this option allows you to target based on the intensity of interest your website visitors show. You'll need to look under the Website Traffic option on the main Custom Audiences screen and select the Custom Combination option.

This will allow you to target any of the following:

- **Frequency.** This will let you see how many times a website visitor performs a particular option—e.g., visiting your website.
- **Dynamic date.** This option lets you target those who have visited the site over a range of dates that you specify.
- **Aggregate values.** Target based on the total time a visitor has spent on your site, or on specific pages of your site.
- **Devices.** Include or exclude visitors based on whether they use Android, iOS, a desktop, or other mobile devices.

Again, if you are still getting acquainted with Custom Audiences, we really recommend sticking with the basic option for now.

A Word About App Activity Custom Audiences

We indicated earlier that, because apps aren't particularly commonplace in dealership marketing endeavors, we're not going to devote much time for App Activity Custom Audiences here—but know that it's an option, and if you do have an app for your dealership, you might want to ask your app developer about this approach.

How to Create an Engagement Custom Audience

This type of Custom Audience will allow you to target Facebook users depending on how they interact with your ads—or, with your dealership's Facebook page.

This is another good option for dealerships who simply don't have the available data for a Customer-based list, or those whose audience on Facebook is still reasonably small. In fact, it provides four basic ways to target users on the basis of audience engagement.

Video Engagement Custom Audiences

If you use a video in your ad, this option will let you target people who either viewed the entirety of the video, or who watched a specified percentage of it. For dealerships doing video advertising, this is a great option, as those who watch significant portions of your online video are going to be good candidates for follow-up.

Lead Ads Engagement Custom Audience

Meanwhile, dealerships that take advantage of Facebook's Lead Ad tool—something we've not gotten into in this book—can engage on that basis.

Canvas Ads Engagement Custom Audience

The same holds true for dealerships who make use of Facebook's Canvas ads option.

Page Engagement Custom Audience

This last one is the one we want to devote some more time to, as it can be extremely beneficial for dealerships who have invested in a solid content marketing endeavor on their Facebook Business page. With Page Engagement Custom Audiences, you can actually target people on the basis of likes, comments, and shares—meaning these metrics really take on usefulness that they might not have otherwise!

When setting up a Page Engagement Custom Audience, there are a few different options you'll get to choose from—including each of the following:

- **Everyone who engaged with your Page.** Choosing this option will create a Custom Audience based on anyone who has viewed your page, engaged with your content, or sent a message to your page using Facebook Messenger.
- **Anyone who visited your Page.** Choosing this option, meanwhile, will create a Custom Audience including anyone who visited your page—regardless of whatever other actions they did or did not take.
- **People who engaged with any post or ad.** Choosing this option will create a Custom Audience including anyone who has engaged with a post or ad—and for these purposes, engagement means likes, reactions (Love, Haha, Wow, Sad, Angry), shared, comments, link clicks... even swiping on carousel-style ads!
- **People who clicked on any call to action button.** If you have a call to action on your Facebook Business page—i.e., Shop Now—this option will create a Custom audience from those who have clicked on those CTA buttons.
- **People who sent a message to your page.** Using this option, you can create a Custom Audience only of those who have messaged your dealership page using Facebook Messenger. This is an especially useful option for dealerships that offer custom service through the Facebook Messenger channel.
- **People who saved your page or any post.** Finally, this option will create a Custom audience based only on those who either saved your page or saved a post on it.

One caveat we should note about all of these Page Engagement Custom Audiences: There have to be *at least* 20 people for the Custom Audience to work, so if your dealership is just getting started with its Facebook endeavors, this may not be the route to go just yet.

Using Lookalike Audiences

An important point to make at this juncture is that Custom Audiences are, generally speaking, about re-engaging with people who have already interacted with your dealership in some form or fashion. They are not necessarily about expanding your audience.

Lookalike Audiences are the exceptions to that. By creating a Lookalike Audience, you'll actually have a chance to go after some Facebook users who *don't even know about your dealership yet*, but whose demographic information suggests they could very likely become your customers. The value in this is huge.

How huge is it? Consider this: You can create a Custom Audience of 1,000 people—past customers from your dealership, for instance—and Facebook can create a Lookalike Audience that has 5,000 or even 10,000 people in it—people very similar to your current customers, ready to be targeted for your Facebook ads!

There are two ways you can create a Lookalike Audience. The first is to create it around people who already like your dealership's Facebook page. The second is to base it on one of the Custom Audiences you have already made—e.g., with your email contact list.

The only potential downside for Lookalike Audiences is that you must focus each one on a particular company—so international businesses that sell their products in many different nations will have to limit their reach a bit. For most dealerships, which have a very focused local presence, this should not be an issue.

Increasing Sales Through a Facebook Lookalike Audience

As for how to effectively use a Lookalike Audience, there are a few options that might make sense for your dealership.

1. **Grow Your Facebook Page.** First, you can target a Lookalike Audience as a way of growing your Facebook page. This is an incredibly efficient way to expand the reach of your Facebook activity, as Facebook does all the guesswork for you. And once you start bringing new people to your dealership's Facebook

page, you can nurture them with daily content—something we'll talk more about in our content marketing chapter—to build brand awareness and also turn them into warm leads.

2. **Increase Leads/ Email Signups.** Alternatively, you can use Lookalike Audiences to coach potentially interested people into signing up for your dealership's email list—a great way to add to that contact list, and an effective way to mine Facebook for leads.

3. **Sell directly.** If you have a Lookalike Audience of locals, you can target them with ads that directly promote your dealership and urge them to come see you about their new car purchase— a great way to directly sell to people who might otherwise not know that your dealership even exists!

Targeting Your Ads to a Custom Audience

Now that we've really gone through the Custom Audience concept, let's circle back around to the topic of *targeting*—because that's really where custom Audiences become useful, after all.

You might remember, from our previous chapter, that after you handle the creative parts of your Facebook ad—the image, the headline, the body text, etc.—you'll have an option to select the Audience. This is where you can select Custom Audience; this should be the first option you see there.

From there, just begin typing the name of the Custom Audience that you wish to use—and you should see it show up as part of the autocomplete list.

From there, hover your mouse over the name of the Custom Audience for a moment, and you should notice a couple of icons appear. One of those icons will just be an X, and clicking it simply deletes the Custom Audience that you've filled in.

The other option, though, is a downward-facing arrow—and clicking that will allow you to *exclude* that Custom Audience, ensuring that the people on that list *do not* see the ad in question.

Using Custom Audiences Effectively

There are, again, a few different ways for you to successfully target Custom Audiences. Briefly, three of the main ways are:

1. Growing the reach of your Facebook page, efficiently and affordably. This goes back to what we said earlier, about Lookalike Audiences.
2. Regaining lost customers, specifically reigniting interest and awareness among those who may have engaged with your page or bought a car from you a long time ago.
3. Selling upgrades or new services to existing customers—whether that means parts, servicing, extended warranties, or upgraded vehicles!

Custom Audiences provide your dealership with even greater control over the people you're trying to reach, and the people on whom you are ultimately spending your advertising dollars. We'll note again the importance of testing in all aspects of your Facebook advertising, of tracking your results and deciding what works and what doesn't.

Here again, though, there are additional ways to make sure you are being judicious in how your ad dollars are spent—and that gets us into bidding and budgeting, the topics of our next chapter.

Chapter 7
Setting Bids and Budgeting

Launching a successful Facebook Ads campaign requires you to make a number of complex decisions—and by this point, you've already made several. You've arrived at key conclusions about your targeting, your messaging, your ad text, and more—and hopefully, you will keep tracking your results and testing your ads, fine-tuning them as you go.

The next big decision you make involves *money*. Every Facebook Ads campaign must have a budget. You are allowed to pay as little as a dollar for a Facebook Ads push, and you can raise that amount by as much as you want. Choosing the right budget for *your campaign* involves weighing a lot of decisions, starting with your own level of skill. When you are brand new to advertising on Facebook, it might make the most sense to work with a more limited budget, but as you grow in skill and precision, you can pay more and get a better return on your investment.

And the concept of *return on investment* is really what all of this boils down to. With well-crafted ads and a finely-honed audience, your ad dollars have a greater chance of actually hitting their targets, which means more customers for your dealership. You don't want to short-change yourself, then, or squander these opportunities by budgeting too small an amount. At the same time, it's important to be mindful of whatever real-world parameters and monetary restrictions your dealership's marketing department is working with.

In this chapter, we will walk you through all the basics of budgeting within Facebook Ads—how to do it properly, what considerations to weigh, and more.

Budgeting for Your Campaign

Before we get any further, though, we need to briefly review some of the key terminology for Facebook Ads—specifically, the concepts of the Campaign, the Ad Set, and the Ads themselves.

The campaign is sort of the big picture; it corresponds with a single advertising objective—like driving more buyers to your dealership website. It is the container in which all your ads and sets are held, and it really has no attributes other than *objective*. In other words, a campaign is distinct for *what you're trying to do with it*—nothing less and nothing more. As such, if you have two goals—to drive traffic to the website but also to increase your dealership's Facebook likes—you will need to start two campaigns, one for each objective.

Budgeting and time scheduling happen at the next level down—at the ad set. Ad sets are defined by their total budget, their start date, and their end time.

The lowest level, then, is the individual ad; ads are contained within ad sets, and ad sets are contained within campaigns. So far, we have spent most of this book dealing with individual ads, but in this chapter we'll look more at ad sets, because that is where the budgeting comes into play.

Now here is why all of this matters. Let's say you have a campaign, and the objective of that campaign is to bring in more website traffic. Within that campaign, you may have two ad sets—one focused on attracting new buyers from your city, and the other focused on attracting new buyers from surrounding suburbs. Facebook allows you to set your budget for each individual ad set—so maybe you want to spend $100 per week on buyers from your city, and just $50 for the suburbs. Facebook Ads makes it easy for you to do so.

Before we get any further, then, we recommend that you give names to each Ad Set to clearly denote which buyer demographics each one targets; that will provide you with clarity as you determine the budgeting for each ad set.

Two Ways to Set Your Budget

Now, there are a couple of different ways in which you can set your budget—either as a daily amount, or as a total amount. So, for instance, you can choose to spend $25 each day for your ad set, or you can choose to spend $200 over the course of the campaign, and then select the start time and end time. Facebook will try to split your budget as evenly as possible over each day of the campaign.

The only real difference here, then, is that if you choose a daily budget you don't have to establish an end date; you can create a continuous campaign and tweak the amount of money you are spending as you go.

A final note: You'll see that Facebook prompts you to set your budget *after* you establish your target audience; it's important to know *who* you are advertising to before you determine *how much* you are going to spend on it!

What About Bidding?

Facebook provides advertisers with a number of options to *bid* on their ads—setting the amount of money you are willing to pay per click, for example. The default setting is for Facebook to handle all of the bidding for you, automatically.

Generally speaking, this is an approach we recommend you stick with, *especially* if you are a beginner. Here's what that will mean, most basically: You'll pay every time your ad is clicked on, but Facebook will analyze the data as your campaign progresses, displaying your ads only to the Facebook users who are deemed most likely to take the desired action from your ad (such as clicking through to your dealership website).

Once you have spent some time working with Facebook Ads and familiarizing yourself with how it all works, you may decide that you are ready to try some manual bidding, specifying exactly how much you are willing to pay per click or per 1,000 impressions. This can be an effective way to contain your Facebook Ads costs, but *only* for those who have some experience.

If you do decide to bid manually, Facebook will offer you both a minimum and a maximum bid suggestion. The closer you can get to the maximum amount, the more likely it is that your total budget will get spent. Remember that this maximum amount just represents the *utmost* you are willing to spend; it is not the specific price you're going to be charged *per se*.

Choosing the Right Budget

When it comes to actually determining the right budget for your dealership's Facebook Ads campaign, there is no magic formula for you to follow; it all hinges on the goals you have for your Facebook Ads campaign. There is no one-size-fits-all option here.

Facebook Ads Budget: The Big Picture

To begin with, remember that ultimately, your aim is to generate profit for your dealership. Whatever else you do when creating your ads, it should always serve this end goal and that means you need to think carefully about how you're going to budget. Yes, spending more on Facebook Ads will ensure that more of your ads get seen, and theoretically you can invest a lot of money into your ads in order to increase the number of hits on your site and therefore the number of sales. The more you spend on ads, the more people come to your site and the more money you make...

Except in reality, it's almost always more complicated than that. For starters, you will likely have a limited budget. Very few dealerships can throw as much money as they want to at Facebook Ads, no matter how effective they believe Facebook Ads can be. Second, it will usually take a small amount of time before you eventually stumble on the best type of ad, with the best targeting and the best script. In other words, you risk wasting a lot of money by blowing your whole budget right away on an ad campaign that isn't at all guaranteed to work.

Starting Small

This is why a smarter strategy is to work out how much budget you have to experiment with and then to gradually increase your ad spending as you become more and more confident in the strategy you're using.

Of course you'll need a bigger budget if you're targeting a bigger niche, too, and for that reason it can make sense to start out with a smaller niche where you can practice and then to move into bigger areas as you start to amass more of a budget to spend and more experience on how to make the most of your ads.

Considering the Customer Lifetime Value

Something else you will want to consider is the customer lifetime value, or CLV.

To work this out, first calculate how much profit you make on each sale. Once you've accounted for CoGS (Cost of Goods Sold; in other words, your overhead costs), how much of the revenue you make is actual profit? Now look at your conversion rates. (Google Analytics can provide you with a good grasp on this information.) When you get 10,000 clicks on your website, how many of those convert into paying customers? If it's 1 percent, then that means you're now getting 100 sales for every 10,000 clicks from your ad. If your cars sell for an average price of $20,000, then you are making around $2,000,000 for 10,000 clicks—not bad at all!

But of course, you also have to divide that number by the amount of money you're paying for each click—and whether it's $1, $5, or $20 makes a world of difference for your bottom line.

Your Facebook Ad Goals

With all of that big-picture stuff said, the first task that you should do in setting your Facebook Ads budget is to simply pause to remind yourself of what your Facebook advertising goals are. There are three basic categories these goals might fall under:

- **Brand awareness.** Are you simply looking to make your dealership more visible? This can be an important goal for a new dealership, in particular, or simply for those that are new to Facebook.
- **Events and specials.** If you are rolling out a new vehicle, or if you have a big promotion going at your dealership, and you want to get some ads churned out in a tight timeframe, Facebook can certainly help you with that.

- **Product placement.** If you are trying to generate some attention for a specific car, meanwhile, there are also tools at your disposal to do *that*.

Think about the *why* of your Facebook Ads endeavor—and from there, you can start to get a good idea of how much you'll need to spend to make your ads effective. We've broken it down into some basic categories below, and we've listed them from the least expensive to the most expensive.

1. **Getting more clicks for your website.** This is the most common goal for dealerships marketing on Facebook, and thankfully one of the most cost-effective. ($)
2. **Generating more engagement for your Facebook posts.** This option entails likes, shares, and comments for your dealership's Facebook posts, which can be key for those whose goal is brand awareness. It can also be quite affordable. ($)
3. **Generating more page likes.** Actually getting people to follow your dealership's Facebook page is a little harder, and a little pricier, though it can certainly be helpful as you try to build an online audience. ($$)
4. **Acquiring more lead form submissions.** If you want to use Facebook's Call to Action functionality to get buyers to actually fill out a form with their contact information, that's probably going to run you the most money. ($$$)

Campaign Scheduling & Audience Size

The next two factors to consider in setting your budget are the *length* of your campaign and also the *audience size* you're going for.

Campaign length—that is, whether you want to budget by day or by campaign lifetime—is something we've already covered in this chapter.

As for audience size, that's where you can really begin getting down to the nitty-gritty of your campaign cost. Indeed, this is the stage at which you'll effectively determine the cost per action—whether that's likes, clicks, impressions, form submissions, or something else.

Generally speaking, a smaller and more narrowly-defined audience (that is, in Facebook parlance, a smaller *reach*) will lead to a higher cost per click, or CPC. Though it may be more expensive, targeted audiences will usually generate more relevant results, e.g., more actions taken from your desired buyers. So there is some trade-off here in terms of expense versus overall value.

To put all of this into perspective, a very large campaign without much targeting to the audience may have clicks as low as eight cents a pop; a more targeted campaign, meanwhile, could run you more like $3.00 or even $4.00 per click. If this sounds pricey, note once again that these clicks will come from more qualified leads and more promising buyers. Note also that this is less expensive than search engine marketing, another big bonus for Facebook Ads.

None of this is to suggest that you need to shoot for either eight cents *or* $4.00 per click; we're just trying to give you some idea of how much you might be spending in order to achieve your desired results through Facebook Ads.

It should be obvious by now that, to determine the cost of your Facebook marketing, you also need to think about reach—and thankfully, Facebook makes it quite easy to see the different targeting options and to get an estimated reach for your campaign.

You can see this information presented to you in real time as you choose your target audience's location, age, gender, and demographic—the basic targeting categories we discussed in an earlier chapter. Narrowing your audience down even further—for instance, choosing the Automotive Behavior option—will provide you with an even more precise estimate of your reach, and thus your cost per click. All of this information will be automatically generated for you by Facebook.

Alternatively, note that using Custom Audiences can provide you with a good sense of reach and total cost; this, too, we've discussed in a previous chapter.

About Facebook's Bidding System

An important thing to understand about Facebook Ads is that, like most other digital ad platforms, Facebook Ads employs an auction system. You don't actually pay outright to run a particular ad, but rather you place a *bid* on available *ad space*.

Because Facebook limits the number of ad shown to any given user, there are restrictions on how many opportunities you'll find for showing ads. This means there is quite a bit of competition, and the automotive advertising space is especially competitive. The good news is that you are *only* competing within your industry, so you don't have to worry about being shut out by large enterprises from other verticals.

Key to understanding this competition is realizing that not everyone on Facebook is actually looking to purchase a car. A lot of different people use Facebook for a lot of different reasons. You are *only* competing with others who want to show ads to your targeted audience—e.g., to car buyers in your geographic area. Those are the people you care about, and those are the people you should have in mind at each stage of the Facebook Ads process—creating buyer personas, creating the ad, targeting, and bidding.

Setting Your Facebook Ad Budget: Some Final Thoughts

We've gone through the weeds here, and we've really burrowed down into the complexities of setting your Facebook Ads budget. Don't let any of this daunt or discourage you, though. If you're still trying to put your finger on exactly what you need to be doing with your Facebook Ads budget, here's our ultimate advice.

Start small.

Remember that you can always add money to your budget down the road, once you have a better feel for what you're doing.

Something else to note: Look at the *frequency* of your Facebook ads. That can be a key indicator as to how you should address your budget. Having a frequency in the range of three to five is what we recommend. If your frequency number is less than three, boost your budget a little. And if it's more than five, either widen your audience a bit or else just end the campaign early.

Additionally, we'll offer these brief notes:

If you have a smaller marketing budget: Facebook Ads work exceedingly well within the context of an integrated marketing plan. They are no replacement for sound SEO or even for content marketing, but they can augment these considerably. We would recommend Facebook Ads *over* search engine ads, which are usually more expensive and won't get results quite as strong.

If you have a larger marketing budget: We still recommend using Facebook Ads, of course, but don't make it too great of a money draw. You never want your spending on Facebook Ads to account for more than a third of your total digital marketing budget.

The whole point of Facebook Ads is to take a highly targeted approach, to spend money reaching a very specifically defined group of buyers. Will that require your dealership to make an investment? Absolutely. Does it give you permission to simply dump a bunch of money into Facebook Ads? No, we wouldn't go that far. Moderation and balance are both keys.

What's Next?

Now that you've learned a little bit more about Facebook Ads budgeting, and about how the bidding system works, you are ready to move on to the next steps. We still have yet to discuss the different types of ad campaigns that are available, including CPA, nor have we fully touched on remarketing with Facebook Pixel. We'll touch on these items, circle back to content marketing, and offer some concluding tips and strategies, all of which we hope will embolden you in your Facebook Ads efforts.

Chapter 8
CPA and the Different Types of Ad Campaign

Not all Facebook ads are created equal. They vary in terms of their content and their targeting, of course, but even more basically than that, Facebook ads can vary by *type*. To understand the different types of Facebook ads, and what they mean for your dealership's ad campaign, it's important that we return once more to the topic of *bidding*.

Before we begin, let us pause to emphasize how important this is. You can write the world's greatest ad copy and you can be meticulous in choosing your targeted audience—but if you have the wrong bidding strategy, and put down too much money on the *wrong kind of ad*, that can effectively nullify everything else you have done. At best, you'll either pay too much for your campaign or you'll unnecessarily limit the kind of audience you could be reaching.

A Quick Review of the Facebook Bidding Process

As we discussed in the last chapter, Facebook Ads uses what is essentially an auction-based system. The process of creating a new ad campaign puts you into competition with countless other advertisers in a vast, global auction.

Of course, Facebook does everything it can to satisfy all of its advertisers, and to provide them with the tools they need to reach their audience—but even on the world's largest social network, space is limited, especially since Facebook caps the number of ads that each user sees each day.

As such, you can't simply pay for ad space outright; you have to bid on it. And those who make the highest bids will get the most impressions.

... or, in some cases, maybe they *won't*. You see, there are three different factors that contribute to the delivery of your ad. One is your bid, but the other two are your *relevance score* and your *estimated action rates*. We'll discuss both of these more in the remainder of the chapter; for now, just make a mental note that having the highest bid does not *guarantee* that you will win. (Skip to the end of the chapter for our advice on how to win your bids!)

As another reminder: The amount you bid for a single click—which is either 1,000 impressions or a conversion—is not necessarily the actual amount you are going to pay. Rather, it is the *maximum* amount you are willing to pay in order to win your bid. Facebook will make you pay the lowest amount possible to win the bid and to get your ad displayed; this is how Google AdWords works, as well.

An Example of How the Bidding System Works

Here is a highly oversimplified explanation of how this bidding system might work. Imagine for a moment that Facebook has three available slots for display ads, and four total advertisers are bidding. Their bids go as follows:

Advertiser #1: Five cents.
Advertiser #2: $1.
Advertiser #3: $1.
Advertiser #4: $5.

Now, it is likely that Advertiser #1 will be left out altogether, receiving very few impressions, if any. The two advertisers in the middle, meanwhile, may get a fair amount of impressions, and they will pay anywhere between six cents and $1 for each of them—but no more than $1. Advertiser #4 will get the most impressions, and he or she will get them for just a few cents above what Advertisers #2 and #3 end up paying—but not the full $10, and probably not even close to that.

The implications here are twofold.

1. Bidding too low is dangerous, because it means you may not get impressions and you may not reach any of your campaign goals.
2. Bidding too much is less of a worry, as you will still end up paying the lowest amount possible. Remember that Advertiser #4 significantly overshot the bidding, but won't actually end up paying anything close to $10 per impression.

Thinking Strategically About Facebook Ads Bidding

In recent years, Facebook Ads has provided more and more options for advertisers—which can be a blessing and a curse. While it is certainly nice to have choices, actually *choosing* is a daunting prospect.

There was a time, for instance, when there were just two ways to bid on Facebook ads—either by clicks or by impressions. Today, though, Facebook's advertising platform allows you to bid within a number of different categories—including CPC, CPM, Conversions, Daily Unique Reach, and more.

Let's devote some time to looking at some of these unique *types* of ads that you can bid on. We'll discuss not only what all these different terms *mean*, but what kind of impact they might have on your Facebook Ads campaign.

CPM Bidding

CPM stands for Cost Per Mille. When you engage in CPM bidding, you are essentially bidding for the *maximum* amount of money you would pay to deliver 1,000 impressions to buyers within your target audience.

This is an inherently unpredictable way of bidding, and it makes it very easy to spend a lot of money without getting many results. That's not to say that CPM doesn't have its place. Larger brands can use it effectively, essentially *blanketing* their geographic area with impressions. For those looking for a more precise and specific result, though, CPM just isn't a great option, and we really don't recommend it for auto dealerships.

CPC Bidding

CPC Bidding, meanwhile, is perhaps the most used of all Facebook bidding strategies—or certainly in the top two or three. It stands for Cost Per Click, and it works similarly to how CPC functions work on other advertising platforms. That is, you only have to pay when a user clicks on your ad.

What this means is that you can have your ad seen by 1,000 people, but if none of them click on it, you won't pay a cent; the worst case scenario is that you end up with a lot of free visibility for your dealership. Meanwhile, if you do end up paying, it's because a potential buyer actually *clicked on something*—and that's usually something you'll be alright paying for!

And by the way: You don't just pay for *any* clicks. Facebook changed its CPC policies in 2015, meaning that advertisers no longer have to pay for comments, shares, "continue reading" clicks, and likes.

Instead, CPC ads will make you pony up only for what Facebook refers to as *link clicks*—which might include:

- Clicks to your dealership website or landing page.
- Call-to-action clicks that lead to a dealership website (like "Shop Now").
- Clicks to install an app (likely not relevant for your dealership).
- Clicks to view a video on a separate website.

Now, as you bid on CPC ads, bear in mind: If your ad has a low relevance score and users simply aren't clicking on it, Facebook may stop delivering it. This is because they want to maximize profits, and after all, it's more beneficial for Facebook to have a one-cent ad that gets 1,000 clicks than a $5 one that only gets clicked five times.

In CPC bidding, then, a key point is this: The higher your click-through-rate (CTR), the lower your CPC will be. That's because higher click-throughs will ultimately lead to higher revenues for Facebook.

Bidding on Conversions, or CPA (Cost Per Action)

Another option you can choose is to bid on conversions. This is sometimes denoted as CPA, which stands for Cost Per Action. If this is the route you go, Facebook will do everything it can to deliver your ads *only* to those target audience members who are seen as the most likely to convert. In other words, Facebook will try to help you fulfill the goals of your ad set.

But what types of conversions are we talking about here? Well, *that* depends on the type of campaign you're running. For instance, if you select the option for a Page Likes campaign, you'll actually be running a campaign where *page likes* are considered to be conversions. If you choose a campaign focused on getting new leads, meanwhile, then a conversion will be exactly that, and so on.

Generally speaking, this is a solid and recommended way to run your Facebook Ads campaign—and the reason for this is simple: Facebook will deliver the ads you create only to the people who are most likely to convert, e.g., the people most likely to take the actions you want them to take.

Now, a couple of notes about cost-per-conversion bidding:

1. Remember that your bid is not the actual price you are paying, but the maximum price you are *willing* to pay for a conversion.
2. Also remember that if you are defining conversions in terms of an external site—e.g., your dealership website—it's important to have Facebook Pixel installed. This is mandatory for Facebook to track the results of your ad delivery. We have already touched on Facebook Pixel, and will get into the weeds with it a bit more in an upcoming chapter.

The Benefits of CPA

We've noted that CPA is generally the type of Facebook Ads bidding we recommend the most, especially to auto dealerships. In this section, we're going to explain *why* that's the case.

Simply put, when you choose CPA bidding, you're removing the risk of your Facebook ads "not working."

Again, CPA means that you aren't paying each time your ad is clicked or seen but instead, you only pay when someone takes a specific action, which you will have chosen at the start.

More Considerations for Your Facebook Ads

At this point it is important to note that Facebook is constantly tweaking its own internal systems and algorithms, and there have been some significant updates to the Facebook Ads platform just in the last few months. We'll highlight a few of them here.

Maximum and Average Bids

Perhaps the most noteworthy change that Facebook has made is this: When you optimize your ad delivery for Conversions—that is, when you go down the CPA route—you can select a style of bidding, and your choices here are Automatic and Manual. If you take the Automatic option—which is the default position—Facebook will essentially handle everything for you. This can certainly be a good approach for beginners.

If you select the Manual option, though, you will notice that Facebook presents you with two further options—either to bid on the Maximum or on the Average.

When you select Average, you're telling Facebook that the amount of money you set is the *average* amount that a conversion is worth to you. Facebook, in turn, will provide results that pretty much stay within the limits of the budget you set, using that average as a guideline.

If this is the option you select, Facebook will implement something called *pacing*, which essentially means that it will avoid blowing your entire marketing budget in the first hour of the day, only to have you miss out on lower-cost conversions later on.

Through pacing, Facebook will provide you with some conversions that are more expensive than your average bid, and also some that are lower—but overall, you'll stay within your budget, and the total amount you are paying on conversions will indeed average out to roughly the number you set.

Maximum bidding, meanwhile, is the option we've discussed elsewhere—that is, bidding for the *maximum* amount you are willing to spend on a conversion.

So how do you know which of these two options to choose?

- **The maximum bid makes the most sense** if your goal is to maximize profits, getting leads at the lowest cost possible.
- **The average bid, meanwhile, makes the most sense** if you're really trying to maximize ad delivery, and get the most conversions possible, and you don't mind if they cost a little bit more.

So, deciding which option makes the most sense for your dealership takes us back to some of the objective-based questions we posed in our chapter on Budgeting. There is no one-size-fits-all answer here.

Viewing and Customizing Your Bidding Options

To view your bidding options—and to change them—you only need to click over to the Budget & Schedule tab, which is found within the Ad Set part of Facebook Ads. This is the menu we've already discussed before, where you can both set your budget and also schedule the start and end dates for your campaign, should you choose to do so.

You may notice, on this menu, that there is a link to Show Advanced Options. This is where you'll go to optimize your ad delivery, do manual bidding (if that's what you want to do), and more.

Choosing Your Optimization

When you choose your ad delivery optimization preference, what you're really doing is choosing which group of people you most want to see your ads. If you optimize for Conversions, for example—the CPA path—Facebook will show your ads to the people it deems most likely to convert. (And Facebook's algorithms for determining this are quite good, we should note.) Meanwhile, if you decide to optimize according to Post Engagement, Facebook will show your ads to users who have liked, commented, or shared your dealership's ads in the past.

The optimization options available to you may vary slightly according to the objective you select at the very beginning of the process. With that said, most ad objectives will allow you to optimize for each of the following:

- **Conversions.** This is the one that we recommend—and incidentally, so does Facebook. This is the way you can typically get the best results for the lowest cost.
- **Link Clicks.** The CPC option. For dealerships looking to get more traffic, either on a landing page or on their dealership Facebook page, this option certainly has value.
- **Impressions.** If you choose this option, you're basically asking Facebook to show your ads to as many people as possible. For dealerships looking to build brand awareness—especially new dealerships, or dealerships that are new to Facebook—this can be an excellent strategy. Note, however, that this means your ads will not be optimized for delivery to the most engaged users. Instead, your ads will simply be shown to members of your audience as many times as possible.
- **Daily Unique Reach.** By choosing this option, you're asking Facebook to *only* deliver ads to each user *once per day*. If you are worried about high ad frequency—that is, of the same person seeing your ad several times throughout the day—this is a good option to curb that. This is an especially good option for remarketing, something we're going to discuss further in a later chapter.
- **Post Engagement.** This is the option to pick if you want to do something like promote a company blog post on Facebook; choosing it means that Facebook will show your ads to the people most likely to engage with your content, i.e. like, comment, or share.
- **Brand Awareness.** Optimizing for brand awareness means showing your ads to the people most likely to pay attention to them—usually a fairly small subset of your target audience.
- **Leads.** This is the optimization approach to take when you want people to share their information somehow—and at the lowest cost possible.

Cost and Optimization

Critically, the optimization choice you make can absolutely impact the cost of your campaign—but how?

To put it simply, the audience members who actually see your ads are going to be different depending on the optimization method you choose. And different audience members won't be as likely to take certain actions as others; some audience members may be very likely to click an ad but not to comment on it, but for others it may be the inverse. This impacts your relevance score as well as action rates, and that in turn influences the cost of your ad.

To put it a little differently, you can show the same ad with two different optimizations, and not only get different results, but also pay a different cost each time. This calls for not only a strategic approach, using the guidelines we've outlined in this chapter, but also some additional testing; it can certainly be worthwhile to experiment with different types of optimization to see what works best for your dealership.

Winning Your Facebook Bids

As we consider all the different types of ad optimization you can select, it makes sense to circle back around to the topic of bidding, and to ask this key question: How can you actually make sure that you *win* your bid, and that the ad you worked so hard on actually gets *shown*?

Remember that Facebook declares the winner of a bid based on three factors—and these factors include:

- **The bid itself.** Since this is an auction, bidding more money means you've got a better shot at winning—plain and simple. Choosing the automatic bidding option will usually mean you do fine, though not always.
- **The relevance score of your ad.** Facebook ultimately wants to maximize its own profits by prioritizing ads people will click on—and that's something reflected in your relevance score. An ad with a higher relevance score is bound to do a little better in the bidding stage.

- **Estimated action rates.** This is just what it sounds like, a number Facebook calculates to project the efficacy of your ad. The algorithms used to determine this are mysterious, and the best way to account for them is to make sure you're doing a good job creating a good, compelling, action-oriented ad.

There is much to think about as you determine the type of ad optimization you want—and it starts with having a clear grasp of your objectives.

One particular type of ad campaign that we haven't touched on here is *remarketing*. To learn more about that, and what it could mean for your dealership, read on to the next chapter.

Chapter 9
Facebook Remarketing

If you've used Google AdWords before, then you might be familiar with the notion of remarketing. Fortunately, Facebook also has its own version of this: The Facebook Pixel (also known as the Customer Audience Pixel). Essentially, this is a cookie that you'll place on your visitors' computers when they're visiting your site. This will then allow you to subsequently identify them on Facebook, thereby seeing whether someone viewing your ad has been to your website before or not.

In this chapter, we're going to go in-depth on remarketing—first looking at what the term entails and why it matters, then revisiting the process of creating your own Facebook Pixel. We'll also provide some specific strategies you can use to implement Facebook Pixel with your Custom Audiences—a powerful way to boost your dealership's Facebook Ads efficacy!

A Closer Look at Remarketing

Chances are, you have encountered remarketing at some point in your life, even if you didn't realize that it went by that name.

For example, have you ever looked at a product on Amazon.com, navigated away from the page without buying it, and then seen that very product following you around the Web—showing up in banner ads on various other websites?

That is an example of Amazon's remarketing efforts in action. And by the way, the fact that the world's largest retailer uses remarketing is proof enough that it works, and that it's something your dealership should invest in.

Remarketing essentially allows you to follow your website visitors around the Web with relevant and related offers. This happens by actually placing a tag, or cookie, on individual site visitors. This triggers your ads to show up on other sites that the user visits, all across the Web.

So, if you're looking at a product somewhere and then you see that very product—or a related one—show up in a Facebook ad, it's not a coincidence. It's just *remarketing*!

Note that remarketing comes in many different forms. Google AdWords, for example, offers some useful remarketing features. For our purposes today, of course, we are going to look solely at how remarketing works on the Facebook Ads network.

How Facebook Remarketing Works

While the Google AdWords remarketing platform allows your ads to be displayed throughout the Google network, Facebook's remarketing tools allow you to show your ads across *Facebook* itself.

Remarketing is closely connected to Custom Audiences, something we'll be getting into more in the later part of this chapter. What this means is that the different types of remarketing closely resemble the various options for Custom Audiences.

You might remember that, back on the Create a Custom Audiences page, you had options to make a Customer List Audience, a Website Traffic Audience, or an App Activity Audience—and all three of those can be forms of remarketing.

-   By making a targeted audience using your Customer List— phone numbers, email addresses, etc.—you can effectively target your ad content to people wherever they are in your sales funnel. This includes targeting ads directly to existing customers, selling them complementary products and services.
-   Website traffic remarketing, meanwhile, is probably the one you're most familiar with, allowing you to target ads specifically to the people who may have visited your dealership's website.
-   You can also target your remarketing efforts to those who have used your app—but again, this is something we are largely going to skip over, with app-based marketing still fairly uncommon among auto dealerships.

Now, you may be wondering: How does website traffic-based remarketing actually work? As we mentioned in our Custom Audiences chapter, the way you effectively tag or "cookie" a website visitor is to use Pixel, which is Facebook's built-in tracking tool. We gave the overview of creating a Pixel before, but now let's look at it in a little more detail.

Creating Your Pixel

In order to create your Facebook Pixel, you'll need to go into the Ads Manager, and then use the Ads Manager menu to click on "Pixels," which is listed under the subheading called "Assets."

If you have not yet created a Pixel, Facebook will automatically prompt you to do so.

You'll need to name your Pixel. Again, this is strictly for your internal purposes, and you only get one Pixel per account anyway, so just naming the Pixel after your dealership should be just fine. There will also be a box for you to check just stating that you agree to all of Facebook's terms and conditions.

From there, Facebook will render a piece of Web code—your Pixel. To use it, you need to include it on every page of your dealership website; if you know much about coding, you'll want to include it in the <head></head> tag.

Adding the Pixel Code to Your Dealership Website

If you have any familiarity at all with HTML, adding the Pixel code to your website should be a simple matter of copying it, then pasting it into the header section of your HTML site. Note that you can go back to the Pixel within Facebook Ads manager any time you need to copy it again.

Alternatively, if you have a Web designer who maintains your site for you, you can simply send the Pixel code to him or her and ask for it to be implemented—something that is usually quite quick and easy to do.

Adding Your Pixel Code to a Wordpress Site

If your dealership uses a self-hosted Wordpress site—which is not at all unlikely, as this is an incredibly popular option—you can add the Pixel code to your site in just a minute or two. There are actually several ways to do so, but what we recommend is going to your Wordpress Control Panel and selecting the Theme Settings option. At the bottom of your Theme Settings page you should see fields where you can insert a Header or Footer. Copy and paste your Pixel code into the Header section, which will ensure that it covers every page of your Wordpress site. Just paste the pixel in there and click *Save*, then you're done.

You can also use a Wordpress plugin to install Pixel. One we recommend is Pixel Caffeine, which is a free download. What you will want to do is go into the General Settings area, then click on Facebook Connect.

After you connect your account, Pixel Caffeine will pull up a list of your Facebook ad accounts and related Pixels. Just select the one you want to use on your website. (You'll likely just have the one to choose from.) Also check in the drop-down menu for Pixel position and make sure you have it set to Head. If so, that's all you need to do. Pixel is implemented, with no copying or pasting required.

Implementing Your Pixel Code Using Google Tag Manager

Another way in which advertisers can install their Pixel code is with Google Tag Manager. You can access this at tagmanager.google.com.

Once you're there, follow these steps:

1. Click the button that says Add a New Tag.
2. Select Tag Configuration, and then Custom HTML.
3. Copy and paste your Pixel code from Facebook.
4. Expand to Advanced Settings, and look for the option that says Tag Firing Options; set it to Once per page.
5. Click the Triggering option below, and make sure you have All Pages selected.
6. From there, just name and save your tag, then publish it—and you're done!

Note that there are other methods available for implementing your Facebook Pixel, but these are the ones that are most likely to be in use by your dealership.

The Best Strategies for Facebook Remarketing

Now that you have installed Pixel, and have also spent some time getting familiar with Facebook's Custom audiences, you're ready to start the remarketing process in earnest—but the question is how.

There is no one way to remarket. In fact, there are a number of different strategies that can be useful for your dealership. We recommend trying different approaches, and, as always, tracking and testing.

In this section, we'll make just a few recommendations for remarketing strategies that we have found to be effective.

Remarketing to All Website Visitors

Under the heading of Website Custom Audiences, you'll see an option for *Anyone who visits your website*, and below it a field where you can input a span of time—for example, you can set it to *Anyone who visits your website* in the last 30 days. Not only is this a Website Custom Audience that we recommend, but it's also Facebook's default setting. This is not without reason: It's a really useful way to remarket.

It's especially useful if you're trying to build your Facebook fan base. After all, people who have visited your website in the last 30 days know what your dealership is and what value it provides; thus, they are more inclined than anyone else to give your dealership's Facebook page a like, and even to interact with the content.

This is also a great way to get people to sign up for your dealership's email list, for all the reasons listed above; pairing this Website Custom Audience with a call-to-action for email signup can be a powerful form of lead generation.

Experimenting with Duration

While the default setting is for you to display ads to those who visited specific Web pages within the last 30 days, we've noted before that this option is variable—and that you can make it go as high as 180 days or as low as a single day.

Though the 30-day default is certainly valuable, there is also value in tinkering with this number, experimenting with different durations.

Your tinkering and your experimentation might even be based on your website statistics. If your site isn't visited frequently—if you get fewer than 10,000 hits per month, maybe—you might have better luck using a longer duration. Meanwhile, you can make your duration even smaller than 30 days, which can be a good option for those with extremely popular websites. (Note that longer durations may cause your ad relevance to drop, which can in turn adversely impact your bidding; do you see how all of this is connected?)

You might even experiment with remarketing to people who visited your website just within the past 24 hours; you'll certainly gain some attention with a message like, *Thanks for visiting our website today. Want to learn more?*

Remarketing by Page or by Category

Something else to notice about Website Custom Audiences is that you can choose to display ads to people who visited specific pages of your website. There are several useful ways to implement this.

One is simply to drive relevant website traffic—for example, pairing ads related to a specific automobile make and model with a website page that is also devoted to that make and model.

You can also extract information from where people shop on your dealership website; for example, if a particular buyer spends a lot of time on your website but only looks at pages devoted to minivans, that might suggest to you that the buyer is interested in a van but hasn't quite decided which one. You can tailor your ads accordingly.

Custom Audiences for Different Landing Pages

Every time you create a new landing page on your dealership website—that is, a page devoted to a specific product, offer, or call to action—you should consider also making a Website Custom Audience for it.

Why? Because for any consumer product, but *especially* for high-priced ones, like automobiles, people usually need some time to think it over before they make a decision.

So, when people visit a landing page but don't close the deal, you can create an "abandoned cart" ad, essentially following them around to keep that particular product fresh in their mind. Your ad copy here should be reassuring, helping instil some confidence in their purchasing decision.

Exclusion through Website Custom Audiences

A lot of our focus so far has been on the Website Custom Audiences to include in your retargeting—but remember that Facebook also gives you options for *excluding* particular audiences.

For example, let's say someone signs up for your dealership's email newsletter; after doing so, he or she is taken to a success page, basically just thanking them for signing up. Because anyone who sees this success page has by definition signed up for the newsletter, there is no reason to include those folks in any future ads that encourage email subscription. You can simply exclude your Website Custom Audience, based on people who have seen the success page, and avoid spending money promoting your newsletter to those who have already signed up for it.

There are other uses for this, too, of course. If you are promoting a particular blog post, you might exclude those who have already seen it—helping focus your advertising efforts only on bringing *new* eyeballs to that particular page.

Using Website Custom Audiences to Re-engage Previous Buyers

Another important way to remarket is to re-engage those who visited your dealership website a long time ago, but haven't lately. This is worth doing, because it allows you to effectively expand your audience with people who already have at least some familiarity with what your dealership does.

You will notice, when creating your Website Custom Audience, that there is a field for including only people who have not visited your website within a certain number of days. Here again, the time period is variable.

What this allows you to do is target ads to people who have visited your website within a certain timeframe—up to 180 days, remember—but who *haven't* visited it within, say, 30 or 45.

Final Thoughts on Remarketing

By using Facebook's Custom Audiences and Pixel applications, your dealership can pursue a *remarketing* campaign—and while this may seem like an added complexity to your overall Facebook Ads approach, the reality is that it allows you a lot more control over who you're targeting ads to, and where in the sales cycle you're engaging them.

The biggest advantage of this is the power of timing. If someone has been looking at your products, whether that means specific cars or more general sections of your dealership website, it's suggestive of a real interest. The buyer in question may ultimately decide that he or she isn't ready to take the plunge, but that doesn't have to be the end of it. With remarketing, you can keep pursuing them, working to build trust and ultimately win their business.

That's the power of remarketing, which is why it's a necessary capstone for your dealership's Facebook Ads endeavor. And with that, we've covered most of the primary components of the Facebook Ads platform.

And yet, there are still a few more discussions worth having—including the important role that content marketing can play in augmenting your Facebook Ads endeavors. We will discuss that in the remaining chapters, while also providing some specific tips and strategies for optimizing and troubleshooting your Facebook Ads campaign.

Chapter 10
Top Tips for Using Facebook Ads Effectively

As you can probably tell, Facebook Ads is a complicated animal—a machine whose parts and systems must be firing on all cylinders, working in tandem, to produce the kinds of results you want on behalf of your dealership.

On a purely technical level, there are a lot of considerations to keep in mind—considerations about budgeting, about ad optimization, about image selection, and more. That's to say nothing of skillsets such as Pixel remarketing, which are unfamiliar to most dealership owners and marketing directors.

But Facebook Advertising isn't just about the technical components. It also involves a lot of creative work. Though there are certainly some guidelines to note and some best practices to follow, composing winsome headlines isn't something that can be reduced to a mathematical formula. In a sense, then, Facebook Ads is part art and part science.

Throughout this book, we have tried offering some basic insights and strategies into how you can not only *use* Facebook Ads to grow your dealership, but how you can use it as effectively and as efficiently as possible.

In this chapter, we're going to codify all of that advice, and condense it into several tips that we'd highly recommend. Consider this a handbook to proper Facebook Ads *strategy*; once you master the technical stuff, use this as a resource to guide your decision-making as well as your creative work.

Note that, in our final chapter, we'll handle all of this from a slightly different angle—*troubleshooting* your Facebook activity when it goes awry. Use that as an additional resource to augment these tips.

Our Guidelines for Optimizing Facebook Ads

Be Up Front and Honest

As we've said previously, truth in advertising is very desirable when you're using Facebook Ads. The offer you make in your ad should never be too good to be true; rather, it should be exactly what you deliver. When a user clicks on your ad, he or she should not be surprised by what they find next.

There are a couple of reasons for this. One of the reasons why transparency matters is that all of your ads are going to be reviewed by the Facebook Ads team before they are approved and displayed. Facebook very much wants to provide its customers (users) with a good experience (relevant content), so they're not going to approve of ads that are misleading or duplicitous. It says as much right there in the Facebook community standards.

But the other reason why honesty is important is that, among its many other uses, Facebook is an incredible tool for *building trust*. Your presence on Facebook can actually have the effect of making buyers more willing and more confident to buy a car from your dealership. But of course, you will undermine that trust if you are dishonest in your advertising. And why would any buyer want to trust their hard-earned money to a dealership that proves itself to be dishonest?

As you make offers in your ads, make sure they are truthful, and also relevant. If you ask people to click on a link in order to save $250 on their next automobile, that link needs to take them to a coupon or promo code for $250—period.

Target Your Audience Narrowly

Here is the basic rule of thumb: The more narrowly and precisely you can target, the fewer wasted clicks you are going to have.

The great aspect of Facebook Ads, after all, is the range of finely-honed targeting options it provides—and if you're not using those, you're not getting optimal use out of your Facebook Ads experience. Rather than pay money to display ads for people who are never going to buy a car from you—people who, from the standpoint of your business, really don't matter—make sure you're only paying money to display your ads for people who are selected because of their high likelihood of heeding your call to action.

We've gone over a range of targeting options that Facebook provides—geographic location, age, sex, and more. These can all be useful filters, ways to make sure your ads are being seen by the people who you've described in your buyer personas. And don't *forget* those buyer personas, either. They can be invaluable guides throughout your Facebook advertising process.

In addition, make sure you take full advantage of the consumer data Facebook provides. Go back to everything we said about the Behavior > Automotive options, which can truly help you to bore down into the buyers most likely to become your paying customers.

In short: Targeting is one of the truly critical parts of this process. Don't overlook it.

Write Headlines That Draw Attention

While you want to avoid getting *everyone* to click indiscriminately, you do also want to ensure that as many people see your ads as possible. Even when you're not selling to someone, letting them see your ad will help to build visibility!

So to that end, try using headlines that garner attention – whether that means they make a bold statement, or they just get people a little curious about something. (But keep in mind our first point, too; your statements can be bold, but still need to be relevant and truthful.)

As for some specific headline writing techniques, we'll offer our cheat sheet:

1. Always keep your headlines focused on value. They shouldn't be about *you*, or what *you* want; they should be about *what's in it for the buyer*. How will they be better off for clicking on your ad or visiting your dealership?
2. Use strong action verbs when you can, encouraging your buyers to take action of their own.

3. Remember that you've got to keep them fairly brief; get straight to the point with your ad copy, especially headlines.
4. Try some different approaches—like asking questions or providing stats and numbers—to see what works; as always, tracking and testing are key.

Your headline is your first impression—your big chance to make your ad effective. As such, writing good headlines should never be a low priority. It should be something you spend as much time on as budgeting, targeting, and these other components of Facebook Ads.

Keep Tabs on Other Dealerships

As you use Facebook, even on a casual or personal basis, pay attention to what other auto dealerships are doing in *their* ads. See what seems to be working and what doesn't. Even spend some time going to other dealership Facebook pages and taking note of headline styles, of which posts seem to generate traction and which ones don't.

We are not suggesting that you copy other ads verbatim. Indeed, doing so can backfire, as you may get reported to Facebook or you may lose the trust of the buyers. Besides, what one dealership does may *not* make sense for your dealership; you've also got to be mindful of your *particular* goals and your *particular* demographics.

With that said, one of the hardest parts of ad creation is getting good ideas—and frankly, one of the best ways to become inspired is to spend some time researching the competition and emulating them where appropriate.

Pick Compelling Images

This falls under the same basic category as writing attention-grabbing headlines. If you want people to take notice of your ads—to actually stop scrolling through their Facebook feed and *read* them—then selecting a good, powerful, striking image is essential.

Now, just like before, we have some specific tips to offer.

1. First and foremost, remember to pick the correct size, ensuring that your ad image doesn't come across looking blurry, warped, out of focus, or otherwise unprofessional. You can refer back to our chapter on ad image sizing for more details here.
2. Think about color schemes. Remember what we said about Facebook's color scheme being blue and white. If you want to stand out, rather than just fade into the background, we highly recommend picking something a little more vibrant, with a little more pop.
3. Remember some of the pictures that garnered the most attention for auto dealership ads—pictures of beautiful cars, yes, but more than that, pictures of smiling and happy customers.
4. Don't be afraid to experiment with images that are more humorous or outlandish in nature, but only if you can make them relevant to your ad somehow. Don't do anything that will risk appearing manipulative or "clickbait-y."
5. Because a big part of the Facebook Ads process is just building awareness for your dealership's brand, it's certainly not a bad idea to incorporate your logo whenever you can.
6. Conveying value through your images—for example, sales prices and discount percentages—can also be effective, so long as you don't make text dominate too much of your ad.

The image you select will take up most of your ad's online real estate—so be judicious and thoughtful in the picture that you select. Make it something that will draw eyeballs to your page.

Test Everything

As we've noted, successful advertising within the Facebook Ads platform requires you to juggle many different factors and concerns—your targeting, your budgeting, your ad optimization choices, your ad headline, your ad body text, the link you include in your ad, the image you select for it, and more.

So what's the proper combination? What's the right balance of ingredients to make your Facebook Ads campaign effective? How do you make sure all the stars align for a truly winsome campaign?

We've offered some guidelines throughout the book, but ultimately, there's not a magic formula for this. There's not a blueprint we can share. There are just too many factors that must be considered, from your overall budget to the demographics of the buyers you're trying to reach. Of course, your advertising goals are also critical.

The only way to find out what works and what doesn't is to *test*. Try different tactics, on small budgets, and track the results. When you come across a combination of factors that seems to work well, make note of it—and maybe put some more money behind it to see if the results improve further.

There is really nothing in Facebook Ads that doesn't bear up to some testing. Experiment, then latch on to whatever seems to work.

Write Compelling Body Text

The headline and the image are what get eyeballs on your ad, yet it's the body text of your ad that ultimately determines whether targeted buyers follow through on your call to action. Writing persuasive body text is another critical step, then, and something that can make or break your ad campaign.

Here again, we'll provide some general guidelines and tips.

1. The overarching concept is to think in terms of value. You don't need text that merely describes your dealership or makes vague overtures to your buyers; you need to directly convey the benefits you can provide, how their lives will improve when they do business with your dealership.
2. Strong action words are once again essential, and can provide your ad copy with the kind of propulsive, forward momentum that it needs.
3. Your ad should always contain a call to action. Tell buyers what you want them to do—whether it's liking your page, signing up for your newsletter, sharing your post, or clicking your link. This is a mandatory ingredient for any good ad, Facebook or otherwise.
4. While your body text will allow you a bit more space than your headline, it is still crucial to be succinct, to get straight to the

point. Remember that most people use Facebook fairly casually, and the amount of attention they're willing to devote to reading your ad is always going to be limited.

Write good copy for your ad. Focus it on value and action. Make it enticing. And test it—retooling your language as much and as often as you need to in order to make your ad stick.

Make Good Landing Pages

The landing page is something that we actually *haven't* talked about much in this book, but it's an important concept to consider as you seek optimal Facebook Ads performance.

Basically, a landing page is a short Web page that is focused on a singular mission—getting the reader to take on particular action. It may be getting the reader to call your dealership and schedule a meeting with a sales rep. It may be getting the reader to sign up for your email list. It may be getting the reader to download a discount code for a new automobile.

Landing pages are helpful because they are specific. Maybe you have a landing page that's designed to get email signups. The landing page should be about that one theme, and that one theme only. There shouldn't be anything else on the page to distract from that one goal, and the page should culminate in a strong call to action.

You won't need landing pages for all Facebook ads. You won't need them for ads that are designed to get more page likes, for example, or to promote post engagement. But for any ad that sends traffic to your website, a landing page is essential—and for a couple of reasons.

The first reason takes us back to our point about keeping your ads straightforward, honest, and relevant. If your ad copy makes one promise, the accompanying link needs to deliver on it. A landing page, as opposed to a more generic dealership page, can ensure that anyone who clicks on your link immediately finds the information he or she was seeking.

Additionally, specific landing pages can be incredibly handy for you as you make Website Custom Audiences, targeting buyers who have shown previous interest in specific landing page offers.

Make a landing page to accompany each of these link-based ads—and ensure that they are short, focused, value-driven, and action-centered.

Don't Forget About Remarketing

Remarketing is vital for any Facebook Ads campaign, something we've stressed in previous chapters. Before you get too far into your Facebook Ads campaign, then, make sure you lay the proper groundwork for remarketing.

This begins with getting your Pixel set up. Remember that, if you need help implementing it, and our resources here don't cover it, you can always get the assistance you need from your Web developer.

But also make sure you have the proper Website Custom Audiences set up. Make sure you have ad copy written not just for new buyers, but for those who have already been to your site. In short, make sure that your dealership's marketing efforts are comprehensive. You won't be able to do that without remarketing.

Be Smart About Bidding

We won't rehash everything that's been said in our chapters on Bidding and Custom Audiences, but we will note once again that there is a very real danger in bidding too low. If you're competing with four other advertisers, and your own bid is significantly lower than all of theirs, there's a pretty good chance you'll get shut out. You may have a great ad, but with low bidding it will never be displayed—and then what good is it?

Conversely, if you bid too high, it's important to remember that you won't necessarily end up paying the full amount; that's just your *maximum*, but the Facebook auction system will only have you pay the minimum amount you need for your ad to be displayed. So, if the other four advertisers in our scenario all bid $5 and you bid $10, you'll likely end up paying a tiny bit over $5—but not the full $10, not even close.

Use Facebook Generally—Not Just for Ads

Facebook Ads should be just *one part* of your Facebook advertising strategy. Combine this with a generally solid social media campaign and make sure you have a good Facebook page with regular posts. Remember that while Facebook Ads can bring people to your page, it's regular content updates that will keep them engaged.

We'll say more about this in our chapter about content marketing; for now, just note that Facebook Ads is *not* a replacement for organic Facebook results.

Invest in High Quality

If you're going to pay for a Facebook ad, then you might as well pay for the design and make the most you can from those adverts. You can find a designer to create you a banner ad relatively cheaply and this will make a big difference to your clicks and conversions.

Remember that your Facebook advertising is about building your brand—and the last thing you want is for your brand to be built on a reputation of sloppiness, poor quality, or a lack of professionalism.

This extends not just to imagery, but even copywriting. Make sure your text is always well-proofed and edited. Hire a professional copywriting service if you're not sure about this.

Approach Facebook Advertising with Care

Ultimately, success in your Facebook marketing will require you to use all the tools we've laid out for you in this book—and while that will take some effort, it's more than possible, and the results can be well worth it.

Chapter 11
What About Content Marketing?

Throughout this book, we have argued for the Facebook Ads platform not only as an invaluable marketing tool for your dealership, but also as one of the top features of Facebook itself. Certainly, it's a big draw for advertisers. No other digital ad platform boasts as many options, or as many unique routes for growing your business.

But is it enough?

That's a little bit of a tough question, as different dealerships have different marketing goals. For some, Facebook Ads may offer a more comprehensive solution than it does for others. Even so, we believe that *all* dealerships should invest in Facebook activity *beyond* just the ad network. This is something we alluded to in the previous chapter.

Why Facebook Ads is Not Sufficient

To explain why, we're going to use an analogy from the world of search engine optimization (SEO). In SEO, there are basically two ways you can make your company website more visible. The first is through creating and optimizing compelling content, which can help you to populate the pages of Google and to reach higher rankings. The second is through paid ads, which can land you placement elsewhere on the Google search results page. To truly cover the page, and take full advantage of all the online real estate Google allows, you need to combine both of these practices, aiming for both organic and paid search results.

This is true in Facebook. Facebook Ads will certainly help you achieve visibility, but it's only one channel for doing so—and to truly have a robust presence, it's crucial to also *earn* a place in newsfeeds by providing valuable, enriching content.

To put it another way: You can use Facebook Ads to effectively build your dealership's audience, and to get a lot more people liking your page. If you don't also post regular content updates to that page, though, then the people who like your page aren't going to have anything to engage with, and your effort will have been wasted.

The bottom line: Facebook Ads is essential, but it's not quite sufficient for a truly robust Facebook strategy. For that, it's imperative to also invest in *content marketing*.

What is Content Marketing?

Content marketing is sometimes described as *selling without selling*. While traditional advertising—and that includes, to a large extent, even Facebook Ads—is all about *you* going to the *buyer*, content marketing is about enticing the *buyer* to come to *you*. And while traditional advertising works through hard sales pitches, content marketing is more about soft selling—providing something of value to your buyers, and trusting that this valuable content will help create a greater sense of loyalty to your brand.

Content marketing hinges on the idea that, if you give away something of value, you'll prove to potential buyers that you know what you're talking about; you'll build thought leadership. Additionally, you'll show that you want to *help* them, which can create trust—necessary for any buyer transaction, but especially pivotal for high-priced items like cars. Finally, content marketing encourages online users to engage and share your content, which can further your brand's visibility.

Again, this is not a replacement for using the Facebook Ads platform, which we believe to be essential. It is a powerful way to augment it though. Use Facebook Ads to bring new users into the fold, then earn their trust and their loyalty by providing them with rich, value-adding content.

Using Facebook to Boost Your Content Marketing

An important distinction to make here is that content marketing is not *just* done on Facebook. Rather, the term encompasses any effort to provide valuable information to clients and leads through blog posts, YouTube videos, white papers, podcasts, or other social media sites.

With that said, the sheer popularity of Facebook makes it an ideal venue for content sharing. In this section, we're going to provide some basic tips for using it *effectively*.

Build a Large Audience

The first step you'll want to take is to make sure you have a strong audience in place; sharing content on Facebook is only effective if there are people there to *see* it, after all.

There are a number of ways you can do this. Facebook Ads is one of the primary methods; we've already talked plenty about how you can use ads to promote your page and harvest more *likes*.

Additionally, Facebook provides a number of useful tools for inviting people to like your page; once you get the page optimized and post a little initial content there—as we discussed in an earlier chapter—make sure to invite your co-workers and other people who support your dealership, and ask for their help in promoting the page.

Publish Your Company Blog Posts

Content marketing works best when you have both *curated* and *original* content to share. We'll get into curation a little bit later. For now, we'll offer some comments on the role of original content.

Original content allows you to share the viewpoint of your dealership—not to directly promote your business *per se*, but rather to build thought leadership; to prove that you know what you're talking about and that you are interested in helping your customers.

The best forum for original content is still the company blog. If your dealership doesn't have a blog, we recommend starting one, and posting updates to it at least once a week.

There are many potential benefits from this, including SEO; Google always rewards websites that feed it fresh content on a regular basis. Additionally, these blog posts can provide you with fodder for your Facebook page. We recommend sharing each blog post as soon as it's posted, and then perhaps once again within the same week; once you build a catalog of older posts, you can also develop a habit of sharing one or two older posts each week, on Facebook as well as other social media channels.

Blog Ideas for Your Dealership

The question is, what should your blog posts be *about*? How do you effectively use this forum for content marketing purposes?

Remember what we said about content marketing before—that it's a matter of *selling without selling*. That doesn't mean you can't occasionally write a blog post showcasing new inventory, or announcing a new line of F&I products, or celebrating an award your dealership wins. You can, and should. Most of your content, though, should focus more on providing *information* that your buyers can use. That's ultimately how you build trust, impart value, and get people to share your content.

Content marketers often talk about the 80/20 rule, which basically means that 80 percent of your content should be informational in nature, while the remaining 20 percent should be more sales-oriented, more straightforwardly promotional. This is generally a ratio that we'd recommend.

As for specific topics of your blog posts, then, think about some of the questions your buyers might be asking as they contemplate a new vehicle—or just after making a new vehicle purchase. Think about the different types of information that might help them to become more confident vehicle owners. Just a few general examples might include:

- Insights and tips for auto maintenance
- Tips for auto cleaning and upkeep
- Suggestions for saving money on auto insurance
- General information about F&I offerings
- Safe driving tips
- Trends in vehicle technology and energy efficiency
- Suggestions for inspecting/comparing potential vehicles

If your goal is to help buyers by providing them with real value, then you're on the right track for blog posts that will do what they're supposed to—establishing trust, building your dealership's credibility, and generating Facebook-worthy content.

More Tips for Sharing Blog Posts on Facebook

As you post your blogs to Facebook, keep these additional pointers in mind:

- Make sure the post itself has an engaging, appealing image in it—the kinds of images we recommended for your Facebook Ads—so that they'll be displayed when you post the link. Images are so critical for generating engagement in Facebook posts.
- Resist the urge to overshare. You can absolutely share the same blog post multiple times, but allow a few days between each share; don't bombard or spam people. Your Facebook followers will tire of that quickly.
- It's smart to write a quick caption or synopsis when you post a blog to Facebook—no more than a sentence or so. Make sure the caption accurately conveys the value readers will find in the most. You might also try asking a question, and letting the blog post serve as the answer.
- The blog's headline is important! Offer a statement of value, ask a question, or frame it as a how-to guide.

Post Images and Videos on Facebook

A good content marketing approach encompasses a variety of content types—not only blog posts, but also photos and videos.

In fact, photos and videos routinely rank as the most liked, most commented on, and most shared types of Facebook content, which means they are ideal for building your dealership's visibility.

There are different ways you can post images and videos to Facebook—either posting directly, syncing up your Facebook and Instagram accounts, or sharing links to videos you upload to YouTube.

Not only do images and videos grab attention, but you can include links to your dealership website (or to an appropriate landing page) right there in your caption.

As with blog posts, we'd recommend consistency, but not excess. A good blend of blog posts, articles, images, and videos is ideal, whereas posting 45 different images in the span of a single day may become wearisome for your Facebook followers.

As for what kinds of images and videos to post, there are plenty of ideas:

- Images of new inventory are always good, especially if you can take the photos in a green area somewhere—somewhere a little less stuffy and formal than your dealership showroom.
- Behind-the-scenes photos of your dealership team members can help to humanize your brand, and allow buyers to feel like they really *know* you.
- Memes and funny images can be quite effective, but make sure you keep them relevant to your brand.
- Infographics—for example, charts regarding vehicle safety or driving trends—can also carry a lot of appeal.
- Videos might include behind-the-scenes tours, quick interviews with team members, video rundowns of new cars, or quick tips/bits of advice from members of your team.

What About Facebook Live?

In recent months, Facebook has really made a big push for its live streaming feature, and in fact it's said repeatedly that Facebook Live streams are prioritized in newsfeeds. Using this technology effectively can be beneficial for your brand, but before you try it out, keep these tips in mind:

- Facebook Live works best when it's casual; think of it as a good way to humanize your dealership, to come across as more friendly and approachable.

- With that said, also remember that it is indeed a *live* broadcast, so you won't get a do-over. Rehearse your comments in advance, if at all possible.
- Broadcast from somewhere where you will be easy to see and hear. The middle of your showroom, where there may be a lot of chatter going on, is probably not the best place.
- Consider using this platform to field questions or just do brief, informal interviews or announcements.
- To make sure people are watching, it's smart to announce live streams in advance, building a little bit of anticipation for them. If you plan on taking questions for half an hour on Friday afternoon, post about it a couple of times earlier in the week, and let people know when to watch for it.

Curating Content

It is important to note that, through content marketing, your goal is to establish trust-based rapports with your Facebook users—and one of the best ways to do this is to provide what marketers call *curated content*.

What do we mean by that phrase? Basically, it's content that you didn't create—and that has no direct connection to your brand—but that nevertheless has some relevance to your dealership, and to your buyers.

For example, maybe you spot a *New York Times* article that speaks to new trends in vehicle technology, a CNN report about saving money on auto insurance, or a *Huffington Post* blog that provides suggestions for vehicle upkeep.

This is all content that could be helpful to your buyers—and sharing it on Facebook shows them that you want to be a real *resource* to them; that you want to help them and support them, not just sell to them.

Curated content should be a significant part of your content marketing strategy, and it can ultimately go a long way toward establishing *your dealership's Facebook page* as a *hub* of trusted information.

Using Facebook Insights

Of course, all marketing activity warrants careful tracking and analytics. Just as Facebook Ads provides you with plenty of information about the efficacy of your campaign, so, too, does Facebook deliver plenty of information about your general content strategy.

Specifically, the tools you'll want to familiarize yourself with include Facebook's Pages Insights and Audience Insights. The point of both of these information sources is to show you more about how your content is resonating with audiences.

Audience Insights, in particular, provides you with a lot of demographic details about the people you're reaching through your organic Facebook content—e.g., your posts, not your ads. This includes basics about gender, age, and geography. All of this information can be absorbed into your Facebook Ads strategy and even used in fine-tuning your buyer personas! It also allows you to hone your content strategy, showing people content that's more targeted to them.

Page Insights are every bit as significant as Audience Insights, as it shows you which of your posts have performed well and which have not. Another useful tidbit from Page Insights: It shows you what time of day your audience is most likely to be online in full force, so you can time your posts to get maximum attention.

Accessing Facebook Insights

Incidentally, accessing your Insights is fairly straightforward. When you're logged into your Facebook account (that is, an account with administrative classification for the dealership Facebook page), just go to the dealership page itself. Right under the Facebook search bar, you'll notice a menu of items that includes Page, Messages, Notification, Insights, and Publishing Tools. Insights is the one you will want to select.

Additional Tips for Using Facebook Insights

As you use Facebook Insights, keep a few further suggestions in mind:

- Facebook will allow you to view the virality of your posts both in general, and also with regard to specific types of posts. For example, you can view which of your posts are most popular overall, or you can look specifically to see which *photo* posts or *video* posts are most popular—helpful when you're trying to fine-tune your content strategy.
- You'll also see a menu where you can see stats on your page likes—demographic insights such as geography, age, gender, etc. This might be useful to you in terms of honing your buyer personas and even in creating Custom Audiences in the Ad Manager.
- Also make sure you look at the information on Reach, which will show you how many people are ultimately seeing and engaging with your posts.

Content Marketing in Summary

As you consider a Facebook Ads campaign for your dealership, we'd recommend pairing it with organic content updates. This may require you to start blogging at your dealership website, and it will certainly require some time and strategy as you gather materials. Maintaining consistent and relevant posts a couple of times each day, however, can be an invaluable augmentation to your ads.

Just remember the key point about content marketing: You're not there to apply a hard sell around the clock, but rather to engage and to build trust. As you consider the content you share on Facebook, just ask yourself: Would my buyers find value in this? Would it benefit them? Would it cause them to view my dealership more favorably? If you can answer yes to those questions, it's probably content worth posting.

A comprehensive Facebook marketing strategy will invariably include both paid and organic efforts. These guidelines should set you on the right path for effective organic reach, but be aware that it will take some time. Content marketing is based on forming relationships, and you can't rush that or obtain overnight results. Be consistent with it, though, and you should see benefits—including benefits to your Facebook Ads activity.

In the next chapter, we're going to return to Facebook Ads for just one more topic—what happens if your strategy just isn't working?

Chapter 12
Troubleshooting Your Facebook Ads

Success in Facebook Ads won't come automatically, and it won't come overnight. There is often some trial and error involved, and as we've said, there are a lot of components you must bring into balance—targeting, budgeting, messaging, and more.

So what happens when you run some ads and they just *don't work?* What happens when you don't get the results you want?

First and foremost, relax. Keep at it. Remember everything we've told you about testing. Just because an ad doesn't generate results doesn't mean it's a waste; usually, you can learn something from *why* it doesn't work. Also remember that, until you land on an approach that does get results, it's best to use a relatively small amount of money.

You can also spend some time troubleshooting your ads. We'll help you out, listing just a few of the most common errors that Facebook Ads novices can make. If you find that your ads aren't netting results, it could be because of one of these issues.

Your Audience Size is Off

One of the first things you might check is the size of your audience. You may have targeted your ad either too narrowly, or not narrowly enough—and in either case, it can throw your ad results off kilter.

A Facebook audience that's too large means you're essentially wasting clicks, which is to say, wasting dollars. If your ads aren't getting any kind of engagement, it might be because you have a very specific message that you're displaying to a very wide audience—in which case you might narrow a little further.

Don't narrow *too* much, though, because that can be problematic in and of itself. While you want your targeting to be precise, and we stand by our claim that narrower is usually better, it is possible to target so much that there's really nobody *left* to see your ads. Make sure you're leaving yourself with some potential buyers to reach.

You're Targeting Buyers Who Just Aren't Interested

This problem can be tough to identify, because on the surface, everything might look perfectly normal. You may have an ad that seems as though it has all the pieces in place, yet when you run it, the results are minimal.

The reason? You don't know your audience quite as well as you think you do, and you're displaying your ads to people who simply aren't interested in them. This could be because some component of your buyer persona is askew; for instance, you might think your client base is middle-class women when really it's more of an upper-price-range product line. Or it could be that you're simply forgetting to take into consideration some crucial part of your demographics.

At the end of the day, the research you put into your buyer persona can make or break your entire Facebook Ads endeavor, because doing it improperly means you're spending a lot of time marketing to people who just aren't going to buy. Make sure you're meticulous not only in composing buyer personas, but in keeping them up to date and using them rigorously.

Your Image Isn't Compelling

We've noted before that image selection is crucial to your Facebook Ads endeavor, for it's what ultimately attracts eyeballs to your ad in the first place. If your ads aren't resonating—if Facebook users are just glossing over them—it may be because the image you've selected isn't an exciting one.

This could manifest in many different ways. Here are just a few of the possibilities:

- Your image is too small, which means it ends up looking grainy, blurry, or warped
- Your image fades into the background, perhaps because of a color scheme too similar to Facebook's blue and white

- Your image simply lacks any appeal; it's boring, stale, or just generally not compelling

If you think your image is to blame, try a high-quality image that includes happy faces—one of the tried and true methods of generating attention in social news feeds.

Also, always be certain that the image you use in your ad meets a threshold for quality, and that it reflects positively on your dealership and its brand.

Your Headline Isn't Compelling

A similar problem comes when you write text for your ad that isn't compelling. Bad body text can sometimes be a problem, especially if you lack a call to action in your ad. More often, though, the issue is with the headline. A bad image means people will just gloss over your ad as they are scrolling through Facebook, and a bad headline has roughly the same effect.

And here again, there are a few different ways in which a headline can go bad. Here are some of the most common headline issues:

- It lacks a compelling verb/sense of action
- It is irrelevant to the offer, or misrepresents the ad content
- It does not convey the benefits you're offering—the what's-in-it-for-me for your buyers
- It doesn't speak to the needs/desires of your target audience

Any of these problems can cause your headline to fall flat, and if the headline falls flat, the ad's not going to do you any good. Devote some time to writing compelling ad copy. If something doesn't land, don't hesitate to go back to the drawing board. And remember to test your headline copy and get a sense of what *kinds* of headlines work for your dealership and its audience.

You Have Issues with Payment

This could be a simple technicality—maybe the credit card you used to pay for your ad has expired. Of course, Facebook will alert you if this happens, and it is a fairly straightforward fix.

The more likely problem is that you're not bidding the proper amount. You may be lowballing, and effectively getting shut out of any chance for your ad to be displayed.

We'll return to the example we used earlier in the book—but this time, let's flip some of the numbers. Say you're in a bidding match with four other advertisers. You bid five cents; the other advertisers bid $1, $1, and $5, respectively.

Your offer here is so far below the others that you're not likely to win any ad displays through the bidding. If you are consistently trying to scrape by with as small an ad bid as possible, you may be sabotaging your own campaign, ensuring that your great ad copy never gets seen or read. Up the ante, if you can, for better results!

You Have Landing Page Issues

Not every Facebook ad needs an accompanying landing page—something we've made clear already. If you are running an ad where the goal is to send traffic to your website, though—and especially if you are promoting a specific product or offer—then having a landing page is usually the smart way to go.

The problem with your ad may be that you're promising people certain information—yet when they click on your ad, they are taken to a generic dealership home page or About Us page. They don't immediately see the information they were promised, so, feeling frustrated, they leave. The solution to this problem, of course, is sending your traffic to a more strategic and focused landing page.

It is also possible that you *have* a landing page, but that it isn't converting. Some common landing page problems include:

- Too much text; usually, short and simple is preferable, and a good landing page is usually between 100 and 300 words

- Not a strong value proposition
- Multiple options or offers; a landing page should be solely focused on *just one entity*
- A headline that doesn't grab attention
- No call to action—the *biggest* landing page mishap of them all

Addressing landing page issues is crucial for any website traffic-based ad objectives.

Your Ad Frequency is Too High

As you set your Facebook ad, you'll have an opportunity to see its frequency. What this means is the number of times the average user in your audience sees your ad. For example, if your audience is 100 people and everyone sees the ad exactly one time, then your frequency will be 1. This is the number you want, because if it gets much higher than that, it means you're showing your ad to the same people over and over again rather than reaching new ones.

As you place your ad bid and set the duration, make sure to keep frequency in mind, as there are always steps you can take to balance that number out and get it closer to 1—bidding more, narrowing your targeting, or running the ad for a longer period of time.

Your Ad Has Gotten Old

Do you ever see a commercial on TV that you think is really funny—but then you see it 100 more times, and it starts to grate on you?

Well, the same goes with your dealership's Facebook ad. If people keep seeing the same ad, you're bound to see its impact diminished. In fact, it can lead some people to feel frustrated with your dealership; it can be a real turn-off.

Stale ads happen when you either run them for too long, or have too high of a frequency. Consider whether either of these might be a problem with your ad campaign.

Conclusions for Facebook Advertisers

We'll close this chapter with two more quick words of advice—big-picture items that can be integral to the ultimate failure or success of your Facebook Ads campaign.

First, we cannot emphasize enough how important it is to test everything—images, headlines, landing pages, ad optimization types, budgets, Custom Audiences, and more. For all the technical options Facebook allows you, the crux of your campaign will involve some grinding, some trial and error as you get a feel for what works and what doesn't within the context of your dealership and your audience. The savvy and effective Facebook advertiser is constantly trying new ideas to see what goes over well.

And the flipside of that is that the savvy and effective Facebook advertiser is *also* diligent in tracking progress. Always be looking at your metrics—using not only the data that Facebook Ads provides you, but also information from your Page Insights, Audience Insights, and even Google Analytics, which you hopefully have installed on your dealership website.

And remember: If your ad campaign isn't working out, there is a reason for it. Do some troubleshooting, do some juggling, and try again. In time, you will come to a strategy that gets results for your dealership.

Conclusion and Summary

Becoming a master of Facebook Ads is not something you're likely to accomplish overnight. There are just too many components, too many moving parts. Plus, here is a secret: Even many professional Facebook Ads practitioners sometimes launch ads that don't get results, or campaigns that go nowhere.

The more you familiarize yourself with the Facebook Ads platform, though, the more adept at it you will become—and the more you will grow in your understanding of what makes for a successful ad.

As you think through your own first efforts at Facebook Ads, let's conclude with a quick synopsis of everything we have learned.

Getting Started with Facebook Ads

Your Facebook Ads journey has to start somewhere—and of course, the first step is making sure your dealership has an official Facebook Business page.

Not only should you create a page for your dealership, but you should optimize it. If you're going to be promoting your dealership via ads, you want to make sure you put your best face forward, and that means having a page that looks reputable and professional.

Spend some time completing your dealership's Facebook business page, optimizing your profile, uploading compelling profile and cover photos, and beginning the process of content creation.

Creating a Buyer Persona

Before you can begin to create ads, you'll first need to have some sense of who you are creating them for. The best way to identify your target audience is to build a buyer persona, which crystalizes some of the key demographic information you're pursuing—geography, age, gender, interests, pain points, values, and so on.

Assembling a viable buyer persona will take some research, but it's well worth it, because it provides you with a snapshot of *exactly* who you are trying to connect with via your Facebook ads—and that enables you to make ads that move beyond generalization.

How to Create Your First Ad

Once you have created buyer personas that represent your target audience, you're ready to create an ad—and that means getting familiar with the Facebook Ads manager.

As you do the creative work of your ad, it's imperative to develop ad copy that grabs attention and ultimately resonates with your target audience—no easy task, especially not with the limited character count you've got. Spend some time thinking critically about the kinds of headlines, value propositions, and calls to action that will work well with your ad.

Facebook Image Guidelines

In addition to the written copy, your ad will also need strong imagery—and selecting a picture that draws attention, powerfully represents your dealership, and also complies with Facebook image guidelines can be a little tricky.

In selecting an image, it's important to pick something relevant to the content of your ad; deception is never a good idea in Facebook Ads. Something that is colorful and visually striking is also recommended. And of course, sticking to the size requirements Facebook gives is necessary for keeping your image looking good and proper.

Facebook Audience Targeting

One of the many great aspects of Facebook Ads is that it allows you to very specifically target your ad to a particular audience. The value in this is that you don't waste money on clicks or impressions from people who will never buy a car from you; rather, you spend every dollar in pursuit of people who *want* to buy from you, or who would at least consider it seriously.

Target your audience according to the demographic guidelines laid out in your buyer personas—and make sure you dig deep into Facebook's data-driven targeting options to ensure real precision in your ad displays.

Custom Audiences

In addition to targeting, Facebook also allows advertisers to build custom audiences. There are many ways in which you can do this, and one is to create an audience based on phone numbers or email addresses from your own dealership contact list.

Additionally, you can create what Facebook calls a Website Custom Audience, allowing you to display ads only to buyers who have already visited your website—that is, buyers who already know about your dealership and have shown an interest in buying from you. These custom audiences can be vitally important ways to nurture leads through the sales cycle.

Setting Bids and Budgeting

How much money will you spend on your Facebook ads? Facebook employs an auction system here, and the amount of money you bid could have a make-or-break effect on your entire campaign.

It's important to remember that your bid represents not the actual amount you will pay, but rather the *maximum* that you are *willing* to pay for clicks and impressions. Lowballing your bid may mean you get shut out by higher bidders, which in turn means your ad simply does not get displayed. Make sure you're strategic in your bidding strategy.

CPA and the Different Types of Ad Campaign

Facebook provides you with various ways to optimize your ads, some of which are more relevant to your dealership's marketing objectives than others. One that we recommend is click per action, or CPA, which is also referred to as conversion-based bidding. What this means is that you essentially pay only for ads that check off one of your marketing goals—so there is basically no risk involved.

Even so, it's important to familiarize yourself with all the different ad types before you choose the one you wish to pursue.

Facebook Remarketing

Something else to consider is remarketing, which Facebook makes fairly easy. Remarketing essentially means displaying your ad to those who have already visited your dealership website, even following them around Facebook with highly targeted messaging.

Facebook's remarketing features are robust, but in order to use them initially, you will need to create and implement a Facebook Pixel. This is basically a tracking code, one that will allow you to keep tabs on the people who have viewed your dealership website. Remarketing is an essential component in any successful Facebook Ads endeavor.

What About Content Marketing?

Though this book has focused primarily on paid ads, Facebook is also an important platform for organic reach—and for a robust content marketing operation. By providing regular content updates that offer real value to your buyers, you can earn their trust and provide them with *confidence* in the vehicle buying process.

Content marketing is a necessary enhancement to your paid ads. Blog posts, images, videos, and even live streams can help you to nurture the lead that you win through your ads, and also to establish the reputation of your auto dealership.

Start Exploring the Possibilities of Facebook Ad Manager Today

Facebook Ads offers limitless possibility for growing the only influence of your dealership—and ultimately for bringing more paying customers to your showroom or lot. Now that you're familiar with the basic features and strategies, the next step is to start exploring. See what you can accomplish through the myriad options offered by Facebook Ads!

NEED ADDITIONAL HELP?

Get My Auto can provide you help with implementing your Facebook Ads campaign or dealership consulting if you'd like to take a more direct route of learning. We look forward to hearing from you if this is the route you choose!

Visit: http://dealers.getmyauto.com

Thank you for reading and I wish you the best of luck in attracting and increasing your leads; then converting those leads into sales which ultimately leads to more profits for you!